What people are saying:

The step-by-step guidelines provided in this book are clearly thought out and you can tell is based on the author's experience of doing lots of photo organizing. Having made a couple of attempts to organize my family's photos I identify with why Bartelt doesn't call the process easy. However, after reading through this guide I definitely feel like I now have a simple road map to follow that can finally get me on my way to getting my photo organizing project completed. – R. Lippert

A useful and needed guide for organizing all my family photos. It is simple, does not overwhelm a person while making sense. – Bailey S.

If you've inherited family photos or you just want to get your own photos organized and digitized, this book is for you. It is well written and easy to read. It provides advice on many different scenarios (family photos, a professional photographer's collection, etc.). As well, the book explains how to incorporate physical photos and digital photos into one organized collection. – Jacki Hollywood Browne, Unclutter.com

Right now, there are about 3,000 pictures on my phone and around 30,000 sitting every which place around my house. No joke, I thought this book was going to be 250 pages, How do you cram all your family life? But this is a easy quick read and super well organized. Bullet points and simple steps. I am excited to pull some tips out and apply them in my own life. – Gina E.

Family photos as a great parenting tool? Yes! This book gives the strategies and encouragement you'll need to use those pictures you've snapped through the years. Feel great about your memories, and strengthen your relationships at the same time."
– Deborah Gilboa, MD, author of *Get the Behavior You Want... Without Being the Parent You Hate!*

The Pixologist's Guide to Organizing and Preserving Your Family Photos

The Pixologist's Guide to Organizing and Preserving Family Photos

Mollie Bartelt

Henschel HAUS Publishing, Inc.
Milwaukee, Wisconsin

HenschelHAUS Publishing, Inc.
2625 S. Greeley St. Suite 201
Milwaukee, WI 53207
www.henschelHAUSbooks.com

HenschelHAUS books may be purchased for educational, business, or sales promotional use. For information, please email info@henschelHAUSbooks.com

ISBN: 978159598-6375
E-ISBN: 978159598-6382
LCCN: 2018947750

DEDICATION

This book is dedicated to my father, David Hartmann, who left this world too soon. His passion for photos and photography lives on in our family.

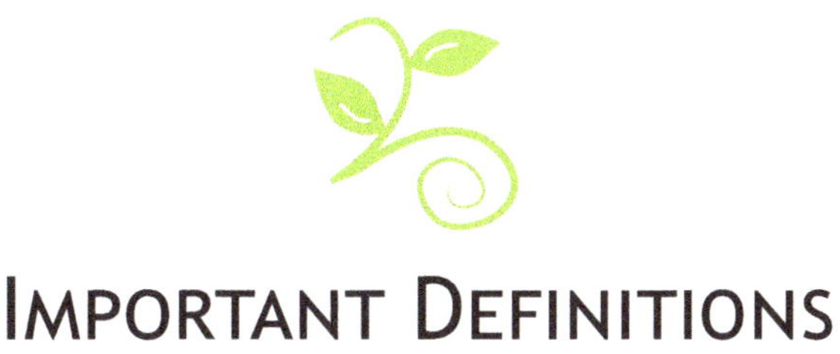

Important Definitions

Pixologie: *The study of life through your photos*

Pixologist: *A professional who helps individuals organize their family photos into a meaningful collection that is saved for future generations*

Saved Photo : *A photo that can be found within a minute or two and has been backed up in two places, one inside the home and one outside the home*

Table of Contents

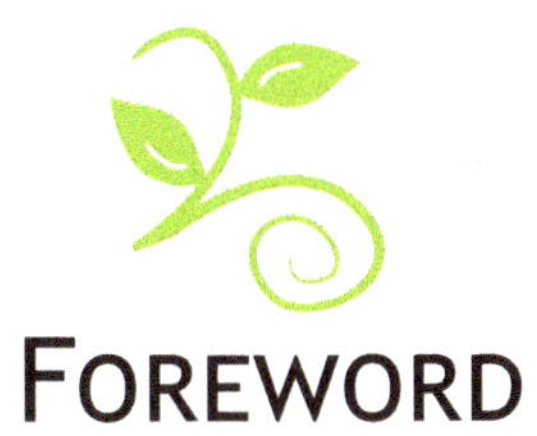

Foreword

She entered my office with a simple lime-green gift bag. The television station's receptionist told me, "The nicest woman just dropped this off for you." The sticker on the bag said "Pixologie—Your Story Matters." Inside there was a crumpled family photograph along with a message about the importance of digitally saving your photos, especially before tornado season.

As a television show host, I had never heard of a photo organizing company but I knew this was perfect timing!

Tornado season was around the corner and the thought of having your family's history blown into the next county was a great "hook" for our audience. Inside the little gift bag, I also found terrific and practical information about how to save your photos and keep your life story organized.

I knew I needed to book these ladies on the show and called Mollie Bartelt from Pixologie to pre-interview her and see if she'd make a good "expert" on TV. Instantly, I felt the passion she had for my own personal photos. She wanted me to get rid of the huge plastic bins I'd been keeping them in and turn my photos into a digital history I could share.

While I was talking with Mollie, an idea hit me! I felt she and Ann would be the perfect guinea pigs for my own

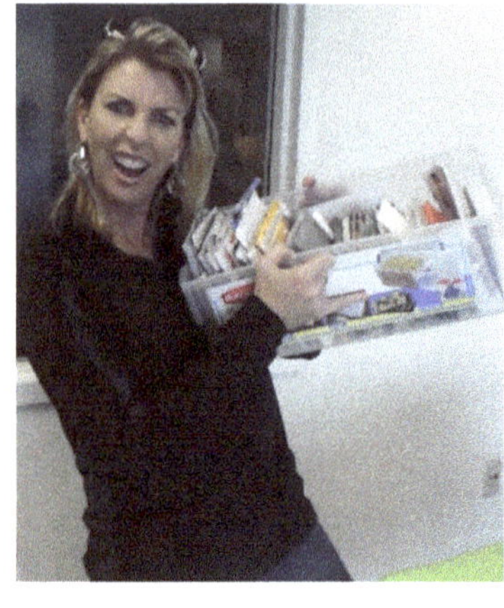

business idea. I now coach entrepreneurs on how to attract the media and be great when the camera comes on.

Thankfully, Mollie and Ann said yes and I came to the Pixologie offices with a photojournalist to help produce what I knew would be a winning segment for our audience. The ladies knew the need to practice for this first television experience, because being on camera isn't natural. There are tricks to make it look easy and Mollie and Ann were quick studies.

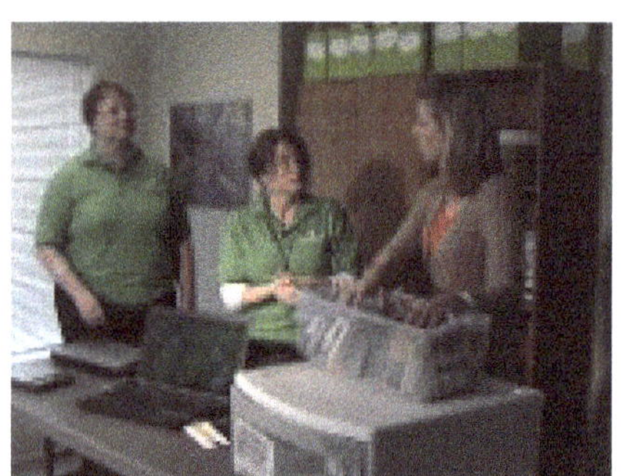

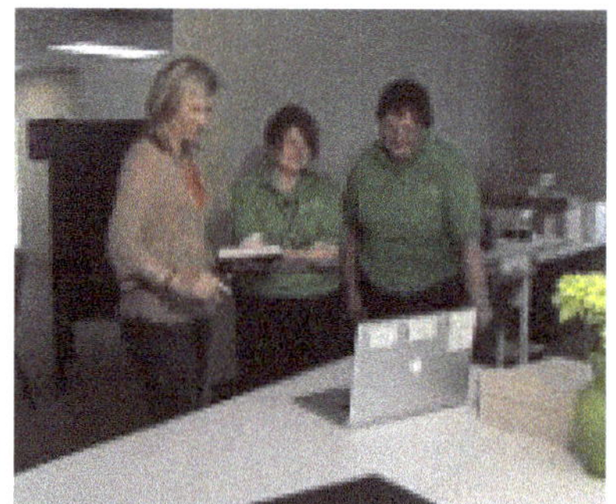

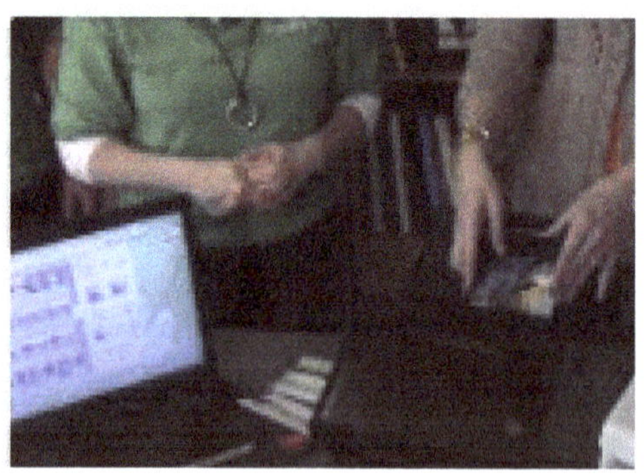

After their segment was done, my co-host came over and told the ladies they were great and had one of the most organized presentations he'd seen. Mollie winked at me with appreciation, but I also knew these were special ladies.

Their passion for your photos is what shines through and I'm so thankful I hired them to clear the clutter of "my story" so I can easily share memories with the people I love.

Just like I did as a young kid and teenager, my son gains confidence from seeing the photos of his family, his growth, and the triumphs in his life and I know your kids will, too.

I'm honored to write the foreword for this book and give mountains of praise for Mollie and Ann of Pixologie, Inc. You're smart for buying this book because the information you're about to read will definitely help you build a lasting digital legacy for your family.

—Katrina Cravy
Speaker and Communications Advisor
www.katrinacravy.com

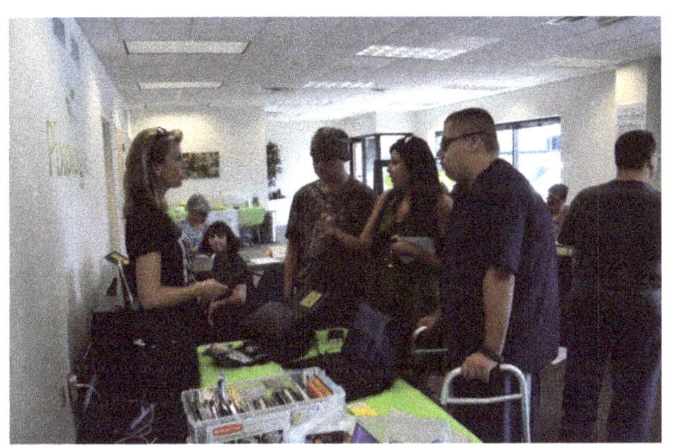

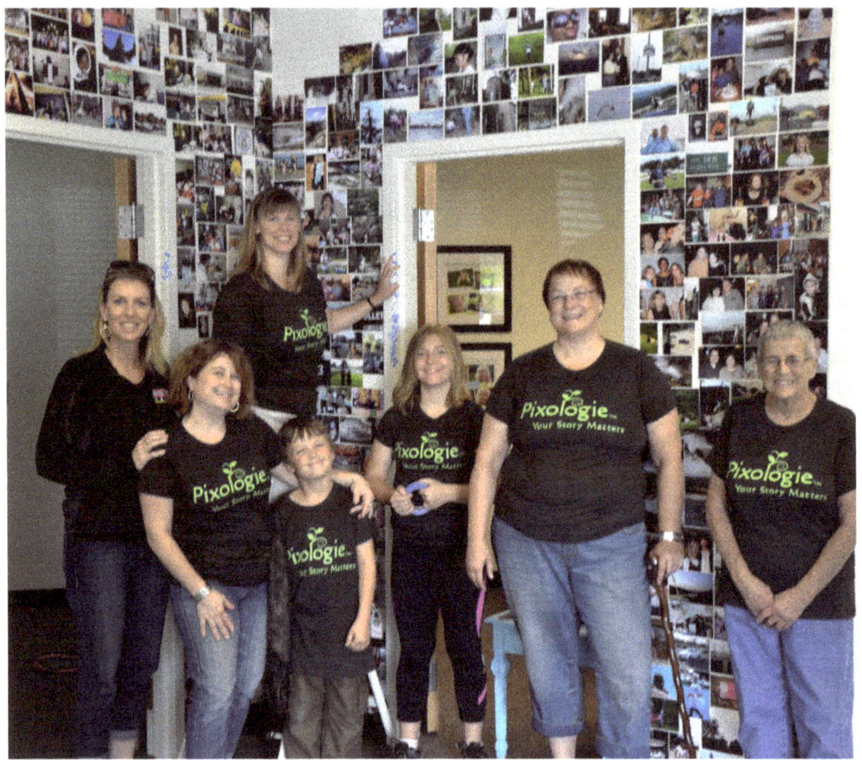

Katrina Cravy helps Pixologie staff celebrate "Save Your Photos" Day.

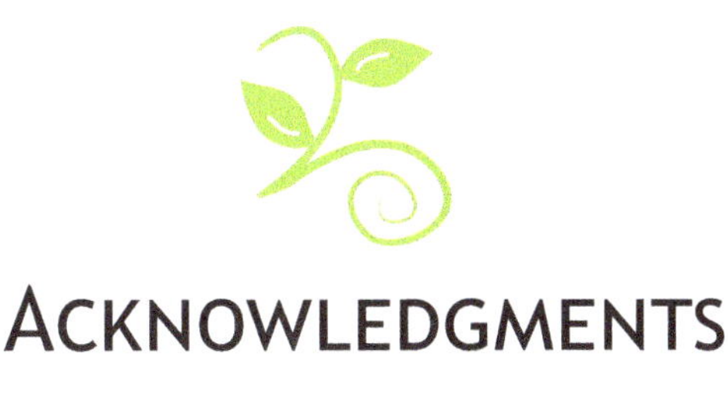

Acknowledgments

This book would not have been possible without the strong and steady support of my husband, Paul Bartelt. He has been my cheerleader, my critic, and my confidante throughout my journey as a photo organizer, author, and business owner.

My mother kept around fifteen photo albums for us kids to look at through the years. Her commitment to saving our family memories helped fuel my love of photos and the importance of preserving them. While she struggles with chronic pain, my mum always has my back. I will forever treasure her words of wisdom, including, "Arise, go forth and conquer!" My sister, Rosie Hartmann, an artist and photographer who jumped on board with me in this journey—thanks for her gritty wisdom and street smarts, which have been so valuable.

Other family members who have been an integral part of this photo organizing journey include my children, Hannah and Alex, who have been ever so patient with me. My mother-in-law, Eileen Bartelt, has been a "hands-on" helper since day one, from helping sort and organize photos to providing commentary on the process, to proofreading and so very much more! Words cannot convey how much she means to me.

Everyone needs a little motivation and I so appreciate my dear friend Tammy Flynn and our Tough Cookie Club. Sometimes you just have to get 'er done and Tammy has been a rock and roll inspiration for me.

My photo organizing journey would not have started without Ann Matuszak. She and I were previously direct-sales consultants with a scrapbooking and digital photobook company that went into bankruptcy. After hearing her vision of helping people organize photos, I was hooked. We dreamed up Pixologie together. Five years later, we have helped countless numbers of people organize, digitize, and "foreverize" their family photos and movies.

I also want to say a special thank you to Katrina Cravy, who, when she was a television reporter, saw a spark of something special with what we were doing in saving people's photos. Her interest in our business led to phenomenal local television coverage and a friendship for years to come.

Lastly, to all the people who have entrusted us with photos, thank you so much for the opportunity to help save your family stories, traditions, and so much more. I truly have learned from each and everyone of you and am so glad you joined us on this ride!

INTRODUCTION

Congratulations! You've taken a big step in purchasing *The Pixologist's Guide to Organizing and Saving Old Family Photos*. Now, your photos have a chance to be looked at once again, and important memories preserved for the future. *The Pixologist's Guide* promises to provide you with a system that will help you tackle your photo mess.

However, that promise comes with more than the price of this book. To be successful at saving your family photos, you must be ready to commit. Time is your commitment. Are you ready to see your photo organization project through to its rewarding end? Many people have good intentions, but never follow through on finishing.

Ever wonder why we put off organizing our photos to another time? Maybe we think a rainy day will come. Perhaps we plan to devote a week's vacation to sorting through and putting our photos in order.

It seems like organizing our photos should be easy, fun, and full of laughter as we go down Memory Lane. But I know the reality is a lot different, as I have found over the years while helping people organize their photos.

As a professional photo organizer and the co-founder of Pixologie, Inc., I've met many men and women who have been saving their photos for a very long time. In fact, saving photos is something most people are quite good at doing. Our clients save their printed pictures in a lot of different places. Any of these sound familiar?

- Shoeboxes, plastic containers, Ziploc bags, envelopes, photo boxes
- Under the bed, tucked in the nightstand or dresser, stacked in closets
- Photo albums (slide-in, magnetic, scrapbook, etc.)

But, are we really saving our photos? I think something prevents many of us from moving forward on getting a handle on our pictures. Let's see if you can figure out what the reason is in these following stories:

- Christine says, "I'd rather do manual labor all day than start organizing my old photos." She wanted to make a photo slideshow for her daughter's upcoming 40th birthday party. A grandmother who travels a lot, Christine described how her daughter's photos were mixed in many albums, boxes, and folders. She had no idea how to start or how she'd make the time.
- Terry brought photos to one of our free scanning events. She said, "I literally had the sweats last night figuring out which pictures to bring for scanning." She laughed, saying she almost needed a Xanax because it was so stressful for her.

- Mary hired us to help organize her photos. During our appointments, she often added new stacks and envelopes of photos to our piles. After two months of sorting and discarding, we scanned 3,768 photos for her. She told me during one of our visits, "There is no way I would ever have finished this without your help."

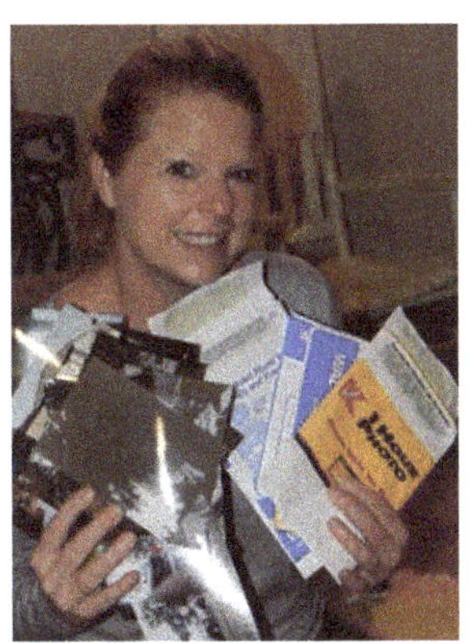

Do you see a common theme in this?

People don't know how or where to start with getting their photos in order.

I wish this weren't the case. Most of our clients find that the reward of completing a photo organization project outweighs the work it takes. But many people never get started, or they start and stop every few years., which just makes a bigger mess to come back to.

That is why I am writing this book—to offer *The Pixologist's Guide* to organize and save old family photos. The system provides a simple way for anyone who wants to get printed photos under control. Then, the memories and stories can be enjoyed, shared and preserved for future generations.

Want to Know What a Pixologist Is?

Back when we first started our photo organization business, my dear clients Bob and Sue Riley were ready to fix their photo mess. They had a walk-in closet full of 55 photo albums, many boxes, portraits, and envelopes. What we call a full-on photo mess. After removing the photos, organizing them with my system, we ended up with about 9,000 photos to scan. Each of their seven adult children received the scanned photos on a jump drive. The Riley's received their photos back in archival boxes.

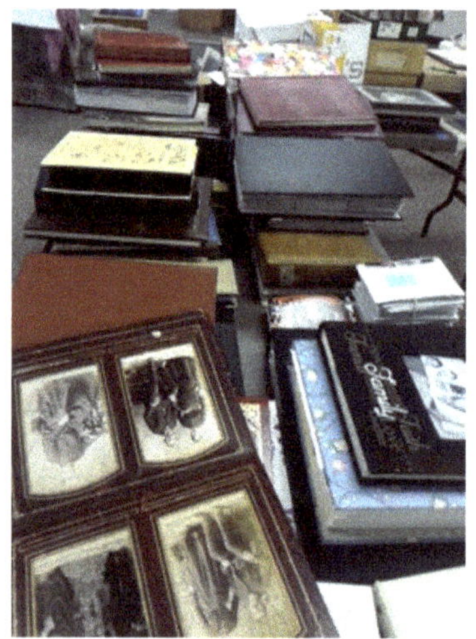

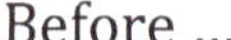

Before ...

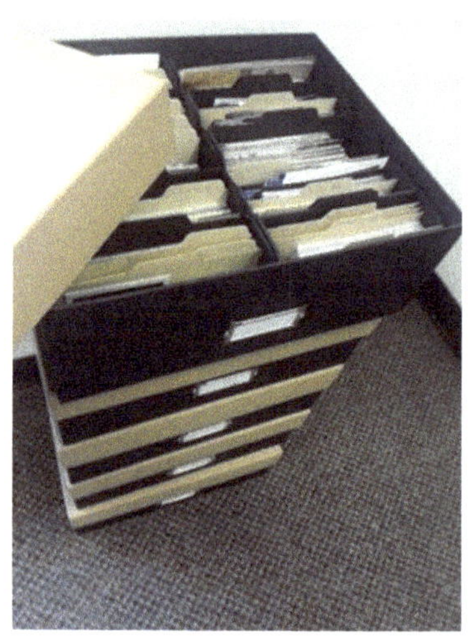

... and after

Because of our business name, Pixologie, Bob, simply amazed, said "You *are* my Pixologist!" For years, I resisted the title, but recently, Bob referred a 79-year-old retired attorney to me.

When she called, she stated, "I need a Pixologist, too!" The woman, Gen, ended up having far more photos than Bob. She also had thousands of slides and negatives, thirty reels of film, and more.

Since then, I am sold on the value a "Pixologist" offers people who need a starting point to tackle their piles of pictures.

So, what makes a person a Pixologist? Good question. Over the years, I have helped organize nearly 1 million photos. If you show me a photo, I can offer you three immediate things to do with the photo.

1. **Toss it**
2. **Save It**
3. **Share It**

Sounds simple, but this is difficult to actually do with the hundreds and thousands of photos people accumulate!

In my mind, a Pixologist demonstrates the following characteristics:

- Knows how to organize photos efficiently and frugally (i.e., saving 15 to 20 of the 100 in a stack)
- Understands which photos will best preserve stories, traditions, and values for next generations
- Teaches people how to organize and save their own photos

- Offers photo organization, digitization, and archival tools that he/she has personally tested
- Provides custom solutions based on a person's technological know-how, time, and financial resources
- *Optional* – Works with family film and video preservation

In short, I believe a Pixologist is an expert in the field of photo and media organization, as well as being very proficient in memory preservation. He or she has put in many hours of work in the field and can answer most any question related to how to save a photo, slide, negative, piece of memorabilia, family film and video, and so much more.

So, the term "photo organizer" just doesn't cover what we do. Some people might call us photo organization coaches, but I like ***Pixologist*** better!

A Little Background

Decades of accumulated photos, slides, and negatives challenge consumers. In addition, the ongoing collection of digital photos being taken today adds to the photo chaos. From a Suite 48 Analytics study entitled "The Photo Management Challenge," here are some industry statistics for you. Take heart and know you are not alone in being overwhelmed by your photos!

- 57% of respondents believe their photo collections either need a lot of work or are largely disorganized.

- If they don't routinely sort through their photos to identify the worthwhile ones, 53 percent are bothered that they don't do this.
- Around 40 percent report not having the discipline to routinely sort through photos.

I see these stats in action every day to an even greater extent. Nine out of ten of the people I meet need some type of help with their photos, whether printed or digital. And if they don't, they know someone who does need support and guidance.

How to Use This Book

I wrote this book in several chapters to set the stage for the multiple phases your photo organization project can go through.

First, I'll share why saving your photos is so important and provide you with additional motivation to complete your photo organization project. Next, I'll outline the tools needed and touch upon which photos should be saved and which should be tossed. Please be prepared—you will need to throw some of your photos away!

Then, I'll walk you through step by step how to organize your photos using the simple system we recommend and teach to our clients.

In the last two chapters, I will discuss how to save your photos and pass your photos on to future generations.

I invite you to skim, reread, and double-check the steps outlined in the book. While the steps are simple, photo organization is not a quick, easy task for most of us. With the system, tips, and tricks outlined in this book, you are well on your way to getting your photos in order.

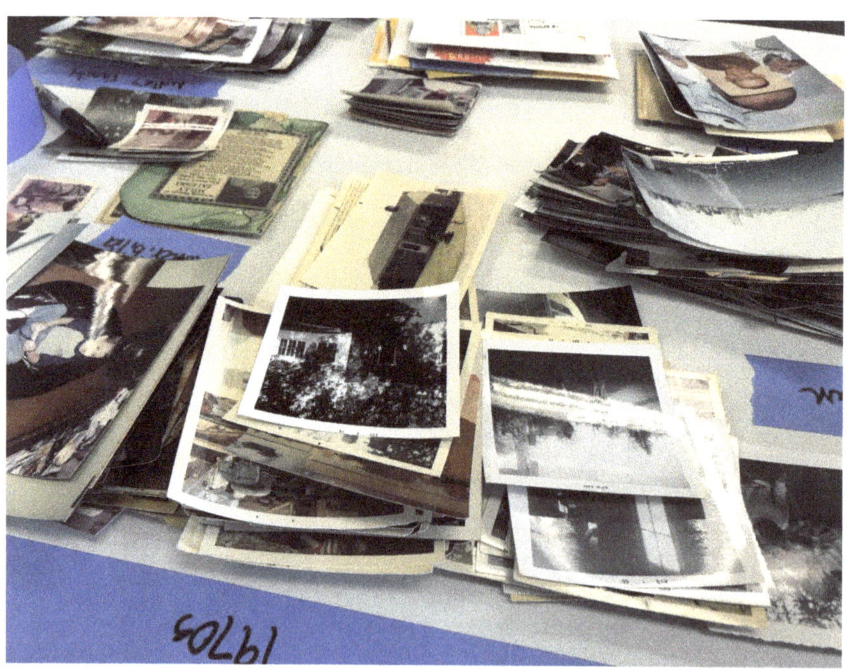

Helpful tips are on the way!

CHAPTER ONE

WHY SAVE YOUR PHOTOS?

I believe wholeheartedly in the power of family photos and preserving the stories captured in those pictures. However, my belief will not motivate you to finish your photo organization project. You must find your own "Why." Write your "Why" down on a sheet of paper and hang it above your work area.

Need some ideas on your "Why?" Let's talk about how photos are so much more than a captured moment in time. Photos inspire, connect generations, strengthen families, build strong children and celebrate life! Let's learn more.

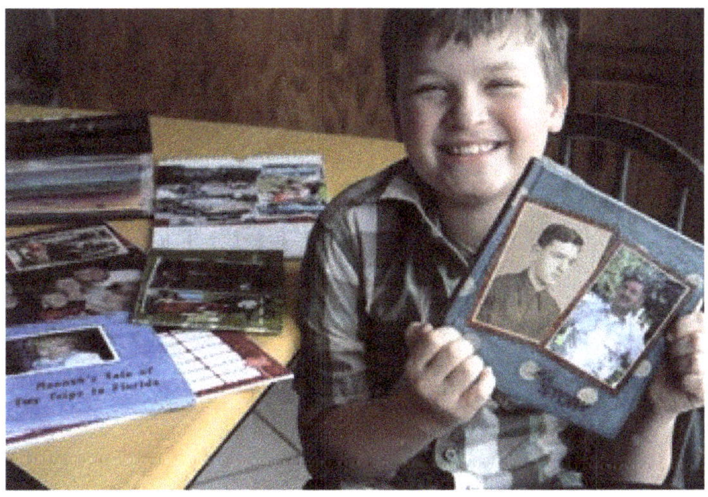

I save my family photos so my children will know their family, traditions, values, and stories.

Photos Inspire

A few years ago at Pixologie, we conducted an informal consumer study to learn how photos impact individuals and families. We found that 70 percent of our respondents stated photos help them get through tough times.

Their inspiring photos included memories such as:

- Completing 50-mile hikes and marathons
- Surviving cancer
- Serving as a missionary in a third-world country
- And many more

Remember Bob Riley, the client who first called me a "Pixologist"? He has inspired many people with his charitable works. Over the years, he has raised hundreds of thousands of dollars for causes such as suicide prevention, homelessness, food kitchens, multiple sclerosis, a Honduran orphanage, and much more.

Here is a photo of Bob at the top of Mount Kilimanjaro a few years ago. This amazing accomplishment involved months of dedicated training. Bob's climb benefitted three charities and raised $60,000 for people in need. This photo captures his spirit, enthusiasm for life, and dedication to helping others. It also shows how perseverance and hard work produce great results!

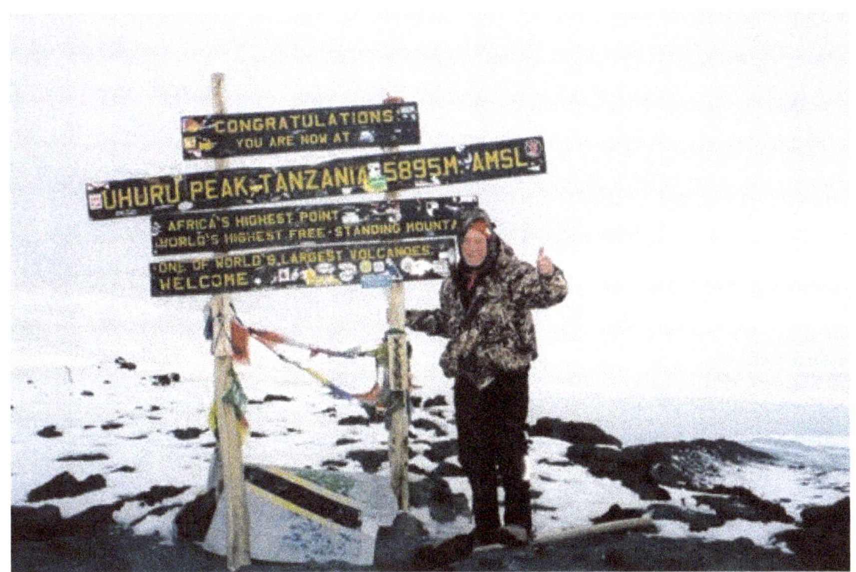

Bob Riley on Mount Kilimanjaro

On a lighter note, I once spoke at a community event about organizing photos. During the class, I asked the attendees how their photos inspired them over the years. One woman mentioned, “Well, they inspire me to lose weight!” What a truth that is!

Photos Strengthen

Okay, you have piles of your family photos in boxes, envelopes, or tucked in bins in the closet. Maybe the photos are on your computer, different camera cards, smartphones, and on Facebook! We know . . . you'll get to sorting out the photos someday. Well, we have some more reasons why you might not want to wait.

Your photos can be an excellent parenting tool in raising happy, well-adjusted children. Parenting and youth development expert, Deborah Gilboa, MD, (also known as Doctor G.) says that "organizing and displaying photographs connects children to our families, our values and our life goals for them."

I was fortunate to take part in a webinar with Doctor G., who explained how this could be. Doctor G. believes that photos impact the three R's of parenting. In her experience, photos:

- Teach Respect
- Show Responsibility
- Build Resiliency

While the events and experiences of childhood help children grow and develop strong values, reflecting back on those moments is important. Parents reinforce what their children have learned by looking at the pictures and talking about the memories.

Teaching Respect—In the photo opposite, we see my daughter, Hannah, feeding a deer. Looking back at the picture, we can help remind our children to treat all life with dignity and respect.

Spend time looking and reminiscing about photos with the important children in your life. You can reinforce the values, stories, and traditions contained within the pictures. If

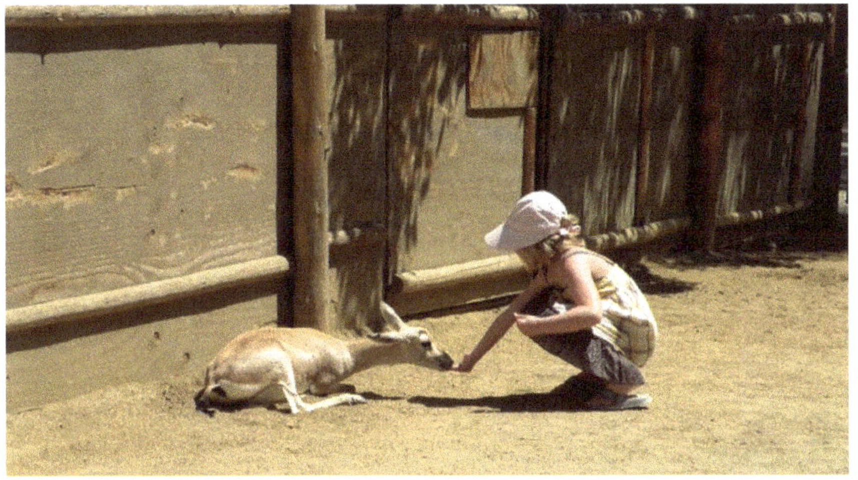

Teaching respect

you don't, there are plenty of societal influences that will fill a child's life and head - and not for the better.

Showing Responsibility —Another time, my daughter wanted to take a kitten home from a petting zoo. It was free, and it was her birthday. But, I had to say no because I didn't think she was ready for the responsibility. We spoke about the kind of care the cat would need, and she reluctantly put him back.

Hannah learned that not every request she asked of her parents was answered positively. She also learned that sometimes taking a pet home isn't the right thing to do, even if it meant the kitten had a warm bed! This moment leads into how photos help children become more resilient.

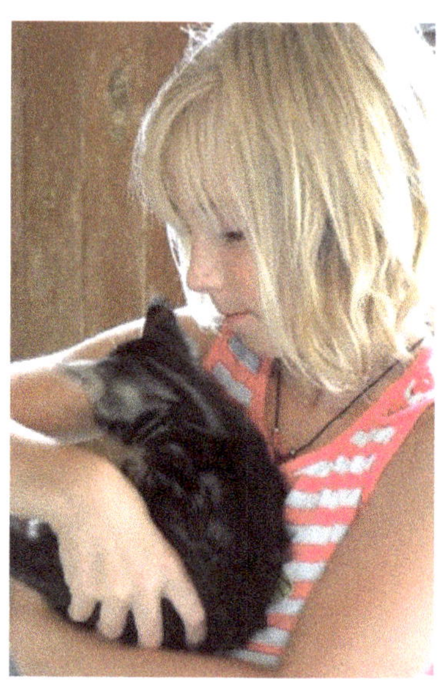
Hannah was heartbroken to leave the kitten behind. Photos help build resiliency in children.

***Building Resiliency*—**As we led Hannah out of the petting zoo, she was sad, even though the day had many fun moments. When children can work through disappointment, they become more resilient to the challenges life throws at them.

I bet you have many memories throughout your photo collection that are teachable moments. When's the last time you looked at those pictures with your children? It's time to get your photos sorted to help grow strong, resilient children.

When we look at divorce statistics across the United States, a staggering number of marriages do not end happily. I understand many marriages require a parting of ways for emotional reasons, among other serious situations.

But, maybe, couples can avoid drifting apart over time by reminiscing over the good times shared together. I believe spending time smiling over photos can help strengthen a marriage, and strengthen the family.

Photos Celebrate Traditions & More

The majority of photos we organize deal with life's celebrations. This includes births, graduations, holidays, weddings, and so much more. Photos hold the key to our traditions and provide an integral link to the past. The celebration of our traditions is extremely important today.

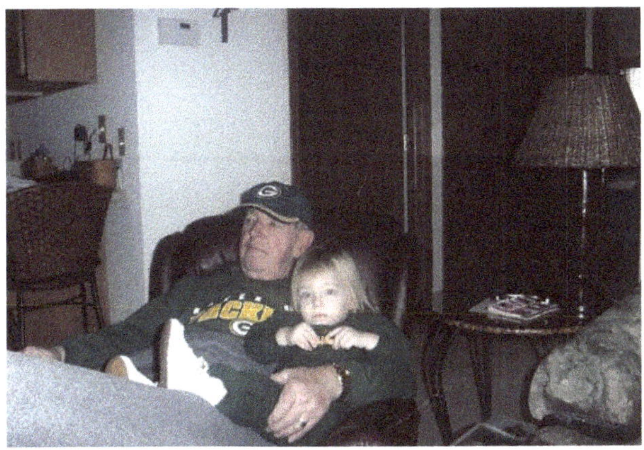

In my home state of Wisconsin, Sunday Packer games are a tradition for us. This photo shows Hannah with her grandfather watching the Packers back in 2004.

Life today in the 2010s is dramatically different from when I grew up with in the 1970s and '80s. There is no comparison to the lifestyles our grandparents lived in the 1930s, '40s and '50s. Our photos from the past show what life was like before the digital revolution.

We need to preserve these photos so our children and their children learn about the important things in life. It used to be that technology brought us together and now it seems to be keep us apart.

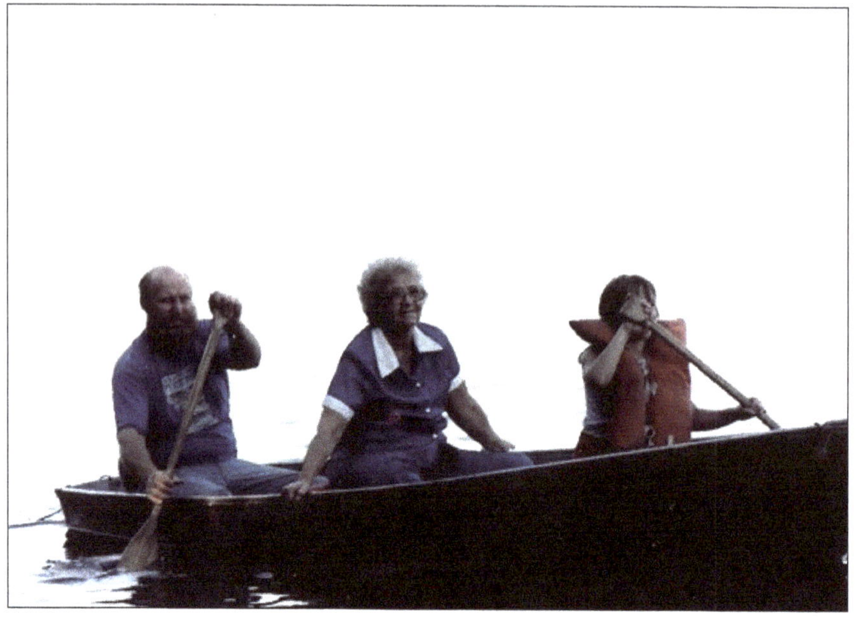

In this photo, you can see my grandmother enjoying a canoe ride up north. This photo is special for a few reasons. Our family loved being up north when I was young. My grandmother wore a dress for all occasions—who would know this in today's casual culture? My sister (in the life jacket) did not remember this moment until she saw the photo a few years ago and it triggered a special memory for her with our grandmother. Life just seemed simpler back then.

Think about the traditions you celebrate and consider where those photos might be. Here are a few traditions and celebrations we hope are in your collection of photos:

- Faith celebrations such as first Communions and Confirmations
- Graduations, family reunions
- Holiday routines including Memorial Day observations or Fourth of July Parades
- School and sporting activities

PHOTOS CONNECT GENERATIONS

In addition to celebrating traditions, photos connect the generations. You can see the world runs differently today than it did years ago. Our children need to hear about where they have come from, what values mattered to their family and how hard work builds character.

Children have greater feelings of connectedness and belonging when they see their parents and grandparents growing up photos. Imagine the impact on children today when fewer than 16 percent of any photos taken are being printed. A full generation is growing up now looking at photos fleetingly on a device screen.

In addition, when completing a family history, I have found that photos are integral to telling a family's story. Photos add impact to family lineages by visually connecting generations. Children, teenagers, and adults enjoy looking back at historical family photos when we take the time to do so. Here is a photo from 1982. Imagine what the baby boy, my cousin Jason, thinks now when he shows this photo to his children.

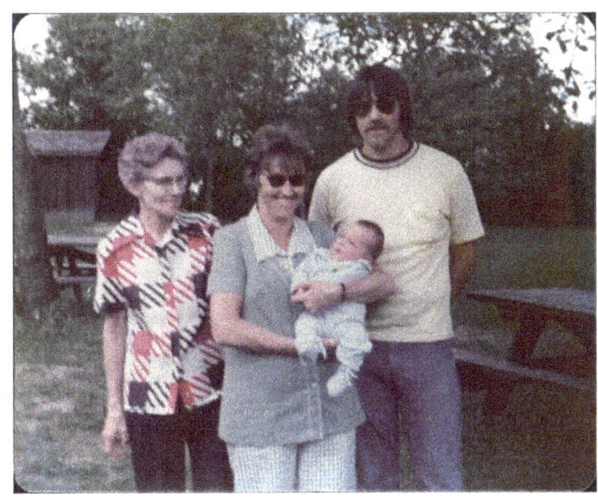

My cousin Jason as a baby with his dad, grandmother, and great-grandmother.

Storm, Fire & Theft

Okay, maybe the emotional rewards of preserving your photos aren't motivating enough. You still aren't feeling the drive to get those photos out of chaos and safely preserved. Let's talk about all the things that can happen to your photos.

Wildfires plague homeowners out west, but a fire can occur anywhere. What is the first thing grabbed when exiting a burning home? Other than children and pets, the photo albums are the priority. Even if the fire is contained and the house saved, water damage to all the contents in the house can ruin a photo collection.

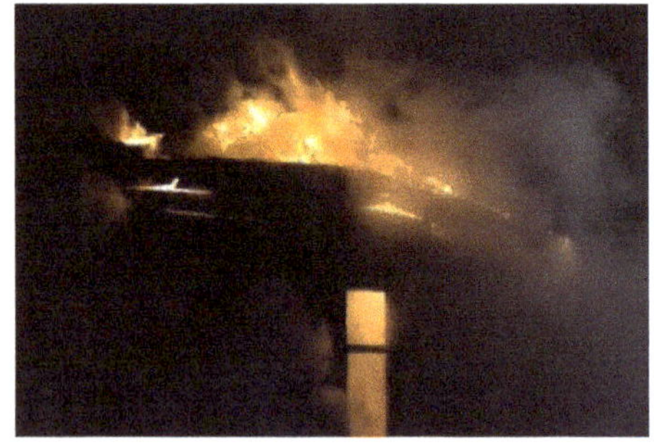

One of my clients experienced a terrible house fire and my husband and I personally hung dry more than 800 photos that had been soaked after surviving the fire. It took us over 20 hours to cut them out of ruined, moldy albums.

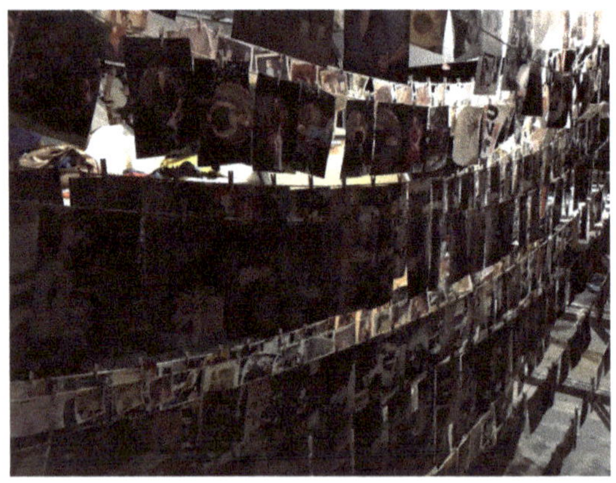

Hundreds of photos hanging to dry after a fire.

Do you live in the Midwest or on one of the coasts? Flooding, tornados, and storms will damage or even steal your photos away forever. I have heard heart-wrenching stories where families have lost important photos and albums. Author and professional organizer Jamie Novak writes in her book, *Keep This, Toss That*:

> *"I can't count the number of people who have reached out to me to share a story of how their photos met with a tragic fate: flooded basement, housefire, mold, or they just became brittle and cracked. Each person felt guilty and regretted not having sorted and preserved their photos sooner."*

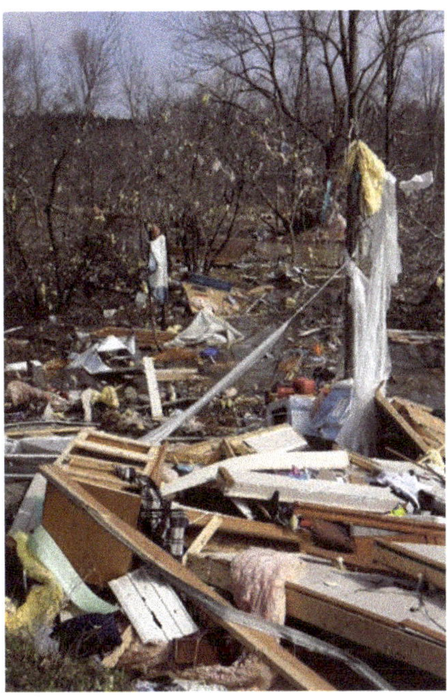

Did you know there is an organization that helps save photos lost in major storms? The National Photo Disaster Rescue organization has saved over 35,000 photos lost in key areas. When tornados hit in Missouri, Texas and Oklahoma, volunteers worked to gather photos from the wreckage, clean them, and return the pictures to their owners.

Learn more about NDPR at www.nationaldisasterphoto-rescue.com.

Don't let a disaster take your photos away from you. If you are reading this book, then you must have some desire to solve your photo mess. Make a plan to start saving your pictures today!

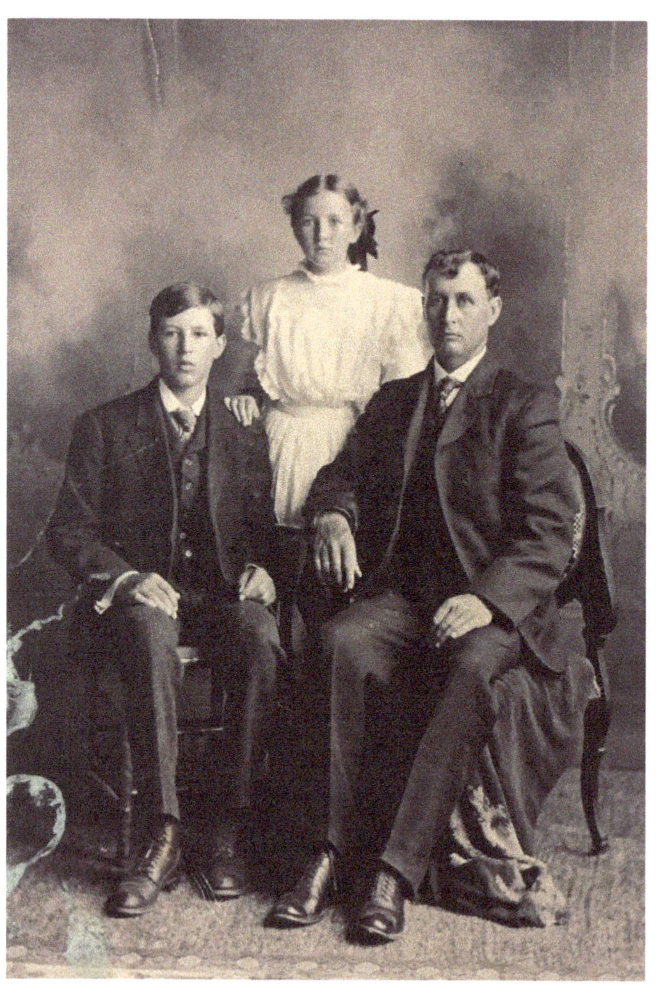

CHAPTER TWO

WHAT YOU NEED TO ORGANIZE YOUR PHOTOS

I'm going to be honest here . . . I did not title this book the "Quick" guide to organizing photos, because rarely is that the case. Organizing photos is a long-term commitment for most people. Even with our help, some of my clients' photo organization projects have taken anywhere from three weeks to six months and more.

This chapter provides you with what you need to get your photos organized: ***Time, Space, and Tools***.

Time Commitment

What is your time frame? Can you commit to working on your photos at least an hour or two every few days? Or a four-hour block on the weekend? Your success in completing your photo organization project depends on your ability to follow through on the necessary steps.

You may want to set a timer for yourself. This will provide you with a set time you work on your photos and may let you know when your time is up. Time flies for me when I am sorting photos, so I need a reminder to stop!

Very important to remember: *this is NOT the time to get caught up in memories*. Take a step back from the personal memories, emotions, and feelings. Once you start reminiscing about a photo, your time commitment grows exponentially.

During the sorting process, people who approach their photos neutrally or even critically will have more success and less frustration.

> While sorting your photos, approaching your photos unemotionally or even critically will save time in the long run.

Have you tried organizing your photos before? Do you have half-started piles from other times you attempted to sort your photos? Let this be the time you finish the organization. We'll give you the system, but in the end, your commitment is the ultimate indicator of success!

Space Required

Sorting through photos can consume a lot of space and time. If possible, you should ensure your space is an area where you can concentrate. The fewer chances for interruptions, the better.

Factors in determining where you will organize your photos include:

- How often can you work on your photos

- How much you need the space for life's other activities (like eating!)
- The ability of your family to leave your designated area alone

Ideally, you will want to have a dedicated table for your photos. A place where your photos can stay out for the duration of your organization project is great. Some people are fortunate in that they can dedicate a whole room to organizing photos.

For working on your photos, you will need:

- A large, flat space such as a kitchen table, but a six- to eight-foot banquet table would be better
- Extra space such as chairs, shelves, or counters to place bins of photos
- Storage shelves in a closet if you don't have room to keep your photos out when not working with them

Due to space limitations and personal preference, some of my clients only bring out their photo bins and boxes while I am there. In these instances, we work on specific sections of photos at a time.

Tools

Having the right tools on hand makes the photo organization process much easier. Here's our list of what you need with more detailed descriptions following.

- A variety of containers
- Long-term, photo-safe boxes
- Index cards
- Sticky notes
- Photo-labeling pencil
- Spatula
- Dental floss
- Gloves
- Blue tape
- Age chart

Containers: Focus first on having the right number of containers for sorting your photos. You will need a variety of containers for short-term sorting, fine-tuning organization, and long-term storage. Examples include old photo boxes, shoe boxes, medium and large bins, wide, open Tupperware containers, and so on.

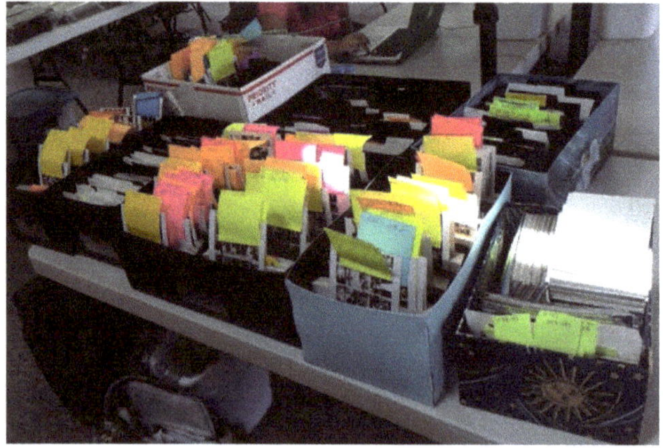

Short-term boxes and bins during sorting process. Also look at the sticky notes being used!

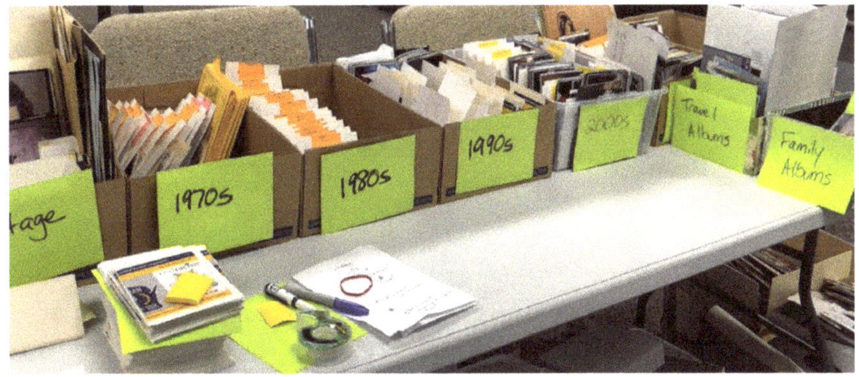

Long-term Storage: Okay, you have a good selection of containers for the sorting process. Some of those containers may be photo safe for the long-term storage of your photos once the organization is complete. If not, you will want to purchase photo-safe, archival-quality boxes.

I like using Legacy Boxes, which hold up to 2,300 photos. These are a true treasure to hand down to the next generation. In some cases, our clients use these boxes for their entire

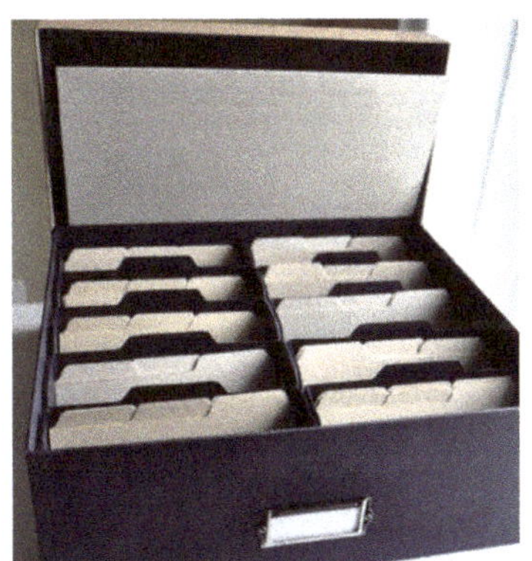

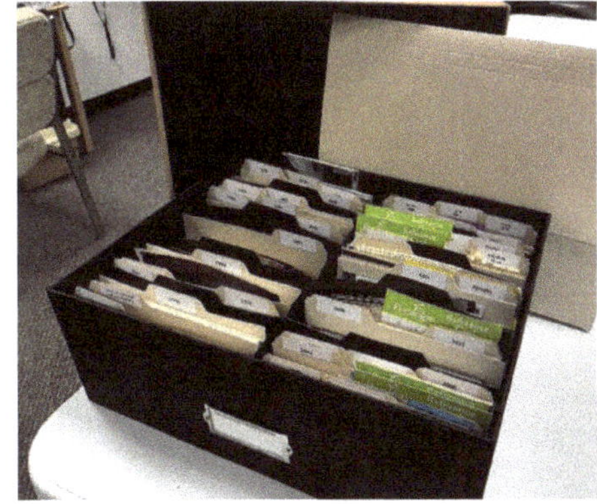

Legacy Boxes: There are ten divider compartments, 60 index cards, along with oversized envelopes to hold larger photos and portraits.

photo-sorting process. The individual compartments and index cards are user-friendly. You will find information to order these boxes in Appendix A: Resources at the end of this book.

Index cards – When stood on end in a container, index cards help section out photos and are extremely useful for sorting photos. You can write on the top of the index card, labeling the section of photos the card precedes.

Sticky notes – We use sticky notes for several tasks, such as labeling boxes and bins with large categories, writing notes on the back of photos, and much more. We recommend having a variety of the 3 x 3-inch size and the 1 x 2-inch size on hand.

Photo-labeling pencil – This gentle, soft pencil provides a photo-safe way to mark the back of photos with dates and the names of any people in the picture. Penciled notes are a more permanent solution than sticky notes.

Spatula and dental floss – When you are removing photos from old, sticky albums, a spatula comes in handy. Carefully slide the blade under the photo.

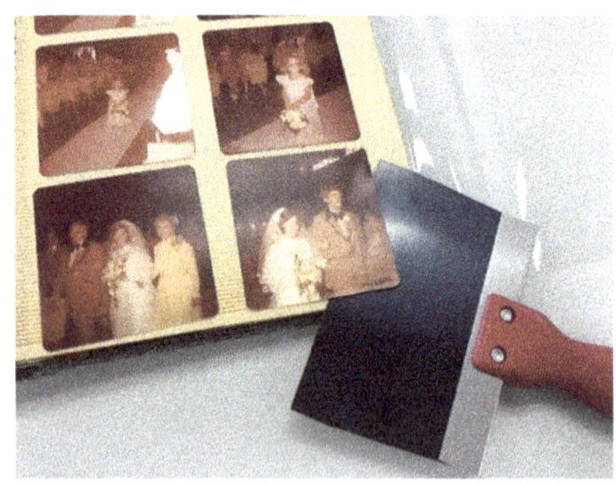

Then, while supporting the photo, pull the page away. Peeling stuck photos out of this type of album results in curled photos that are difficult to scan. For more precision, use dental floss to do the same task.

Gloves – You can buy white, cotton gloves from a variety of places. When you handle old photos that are crumbling, fragile, and delicate, gloves are a must. The oils from your hands and fingers will damage the photo further, risking a tear, stain, or more. Using gloves may prevent the need for an expensive photo restoration of an important heritage photo. In addition, the gloves protect your hands from mold, grime, and other substances that may be on old photos.

Blue tape – Oh, how we love our blue painter's tape! We use this generously at our studio to help photo-sorting clients divide a table into sections. Then we label the tape with categories to help organize photos further. The tape doesn't stick permanently and provides a clear visual for clients who need direction on how to start sorting photos.

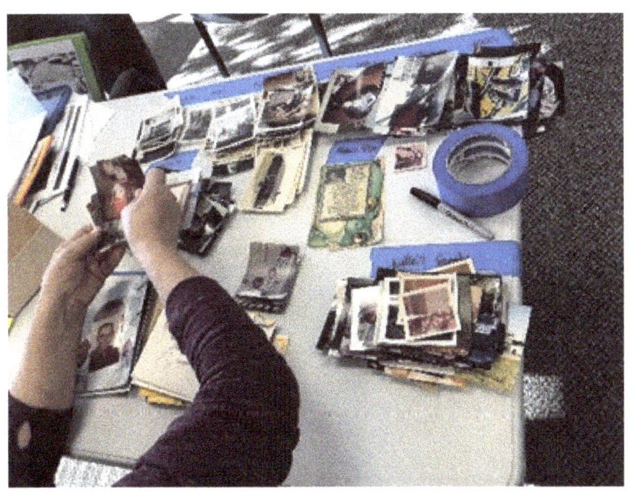

Age chart – This tool provides ESSENTIAL clues to dating pictures, especially for those people who have children. One of my clients has four children – all of whom had a birthday party every year. I couldn't imagine helping her with her photos without the age chart. Here's an example of an age chart:

Year	Child #1 – Mollie		Child #2 - Rosie	
	Age	Grade	Age	Grade
1972	Born 9/3/1972			
1973	1			
1974	2		Born 7/1/1974	
1975	3		1	
1976	4		2	
1977	5	Preschool	3	
1978	6	Preschool/1st	4	
1979	7	First/Second	5	Preschool
1980	8	Second/Third	6	Preschool/1st
1981	9	Third/Fourth	7	First/Second
1982	10	Fourth/Fifth	8	Second/Third
1983	11	Fifth/Sixth	9	Third/Fourth
1984	12	Sixth/Seventh	10	Fourth/Fifth
1985	13	Seventh/Eighth	11	Fifth/Sixth
1986	14	Eighth/Freshman	12	Sixth/Seventh
1987	15	Freshman/Sophomore	13	Seventh/Eighth
1988	16	Sophomore/Junior	14	Eighth/Freshman
1989	17	Junior/Senior	15	Freshman/Sophomore
1990	18	Senior – Graduated HS	16	Sophomore/Junior
1991	19		17	Junior/Senior
1992	20		18	Senior – Graduated HS
Other Milestones	1994 – Graduated College 1996 - Wedding		1998 - Wedding	

You can find a customizable Age Chart at www.pixologieinc.com under Tools.

Keep in mind that the school year spans two years. For this age chart, I used the year the child started that grade. For example, at age 15, Mollie entered her freshman year in high school in 1987. Photos of her in her freshman year, however, may span from September 1987 to June of 1988.

Find clues in your photos that might help date the photo. In the photo below of young me, there are ten candles on the birthday cake. Looking at the age chart, I can see that I turned ten in 1982.

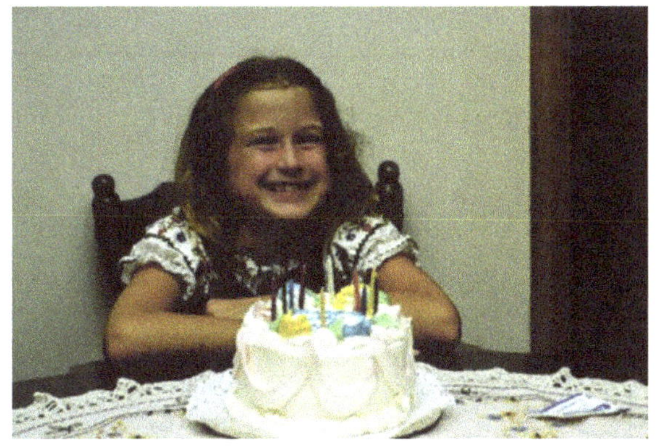

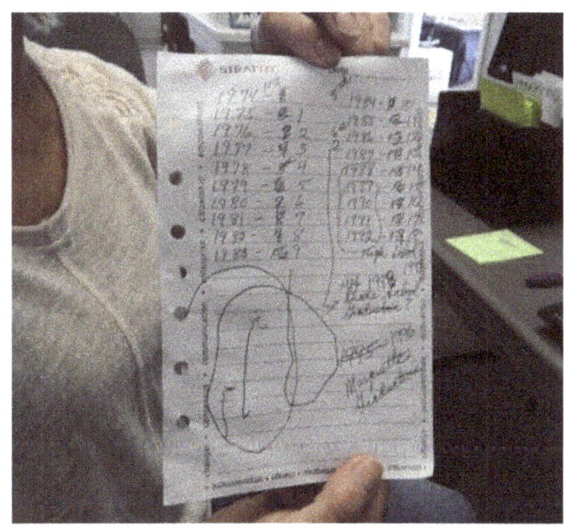

Here's an example of a handwritten age chart.

If you are organizing a large collection of photos with multiple families, a more expansive timeline may be required. Just apply the same principles of known dates and events (weddings, funerals, immigration dates, etc.)

Okay, we've covered the topics of time, space and tools. Now, we can dive into what photos you should save and then how to organize your photos!

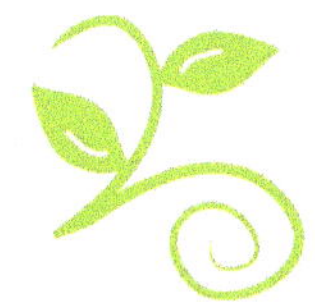

CHAPTER THREE

WHICH PHOTOS SHOULD YOU KEEP?

Want to be successful in your photo organizing efforts? Have a clear goal in mind of what you want to save? And, then brace yourself for the inevitable. . . you will need to be OKAY with throwing away photos. Not only that, if you want to finish this project in a reasonable amount of time (not years!), you will need to make quick decisions on what to keep and what to let go.

For some people, this is extremely difficult, and others find it therapeutic. This chapter gives you strong permission to keep the photos you absolutely love and to get rid of photos that you don't need.

Some people ask for a specific number of photos they should save. Unfortunately, no magic formula exists on how many photos to save. It is also hard to picture (sorry for the pun!) what different quantities of photos look like. Based on experiences with my clients, here are some guidelines.

- One standard shoebox holds approximately 1,000 photos.
- A frugal, efficient photo sorter will have one shoebox for each decade—roughly 100 photos per year. This number of photos will capture a good section of the important times in your life.

- A passionate, emotionally attached photo sorter will save approximately one shoebox for every two years. This means one decade will have 5,000 photos. In today's society, where we can take more than 5,000 photos in one year, that doesn't seem like a lot!
- And there is everything in between. No right or wrong answer here!

In her book *Downsizing the Family Home*, author Marni Jameson writes,

> *"The goal of photos is to preserve memories, but no one wants to look through all the unedited photos of a lifetime."*

Think of your role here as curator. You will pull the best photos and stories out of a generation or more of photos for future generations to be able to enjoy. How many photos can you look at and enjoy in one afternoon when the family gathers together?

The number of photos saved differs depending upon each person. A couple of examples include:

- Mary's Photo Organizing Project—3,486 photos spanning the years 1910 to 2010
- Bob's Photo Organizing Project—9,500 photos spanning from the late 1800s to early 2000s
- Ken's Photo Organizing Project —26,452 photos spanning the 1930s to early 2000s

General Recommendations for Which Photos To Save

My "what to save" recommendations refer to photo collections in general. I have found that sometimes bad photos are the most precious to keep. So, with that being said, please use your heart and your judgment in determining what you want to save. Keep every photo you absolutely love, even if it is of poor quality.

I offer the following points for you to think about which photos you can keep and which photos you can toss.

1. **Identifiable people.** Does your photo contain friends, family members, and other acquaintances you know and want to remember?

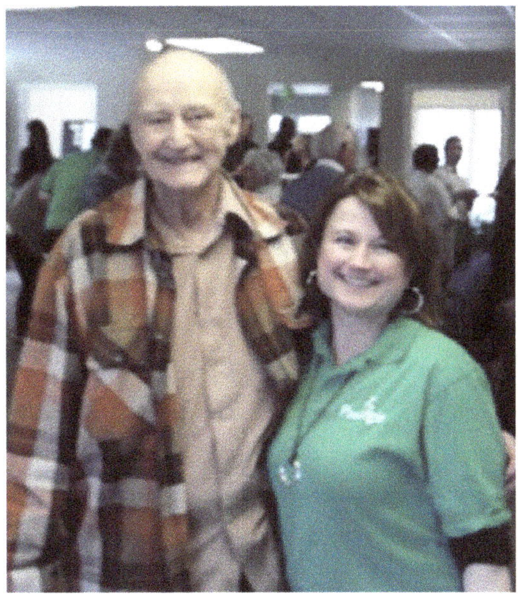

This photo of my dad and me is blurry and I wish it were clearer. However, he's gone now and I will treasure it always as it was the grand opening day of our business. He was there to celebrate with us.

Examples of photos you can toss: crowd settings where no one is recognizable and school activity photos where you cannot see your children.

2. **Landscape, vacation, photos of flowers, trips to the zoo**, etc. Save if your photo contains family in it or a meaningful moment that you remember.

   Examples of photos you may want to toss: landscape scenes you don't recall, vacation photos that are repetitive, most every zoo photo taken without a family member in the picture. Back in a 2007 trip to Florida, I had to laugh at this because I took a photo of nearly every animal at Disney World's Animal Kingdom. I saved the two or three best animal photos and tossed the rest.

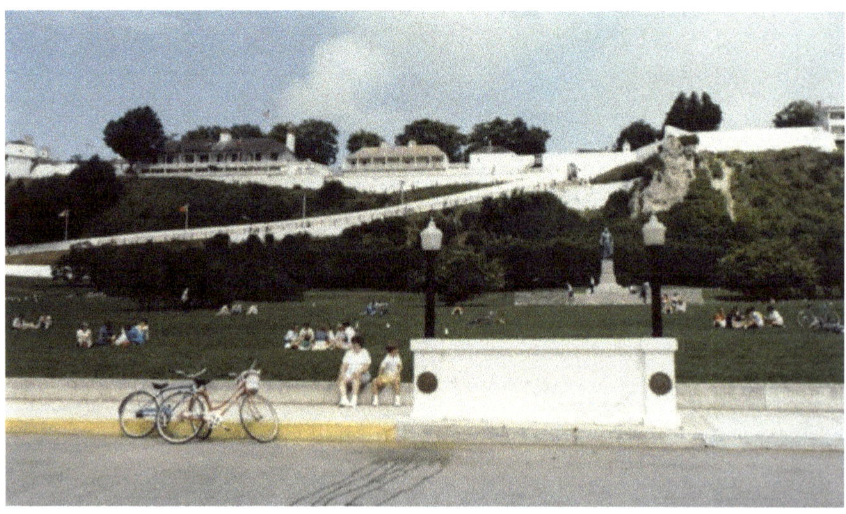

This photo is a prime example of one that can be tossed. It was taken on Mackinac Island and I believe it is the Grand Hotel or grounds surrounding it. My mom, dad, sister, and I rode our bikes around the island and this photo captures nothing of those hours we spent. However, the photo opposite of my sister says so much!

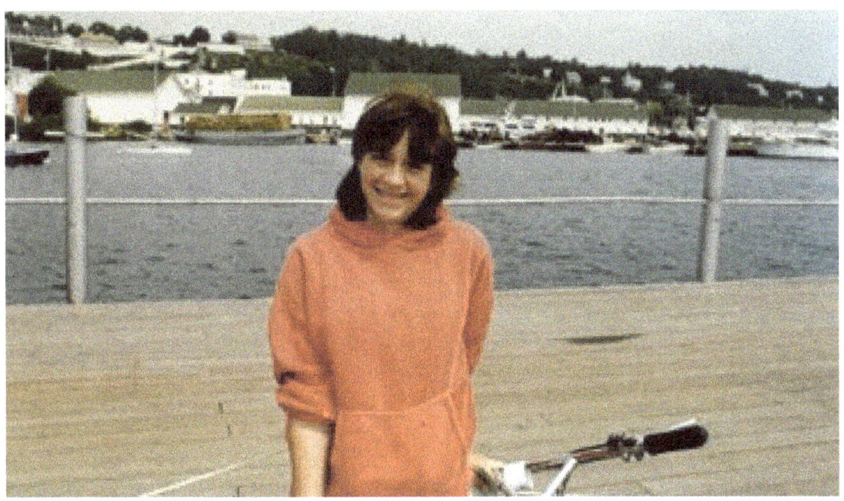

Happy moments before the teen years of rebellion, family arguments, and more make me smile. If I didn't have this photo, I wouldn't remember that we had some great times on that road trip.

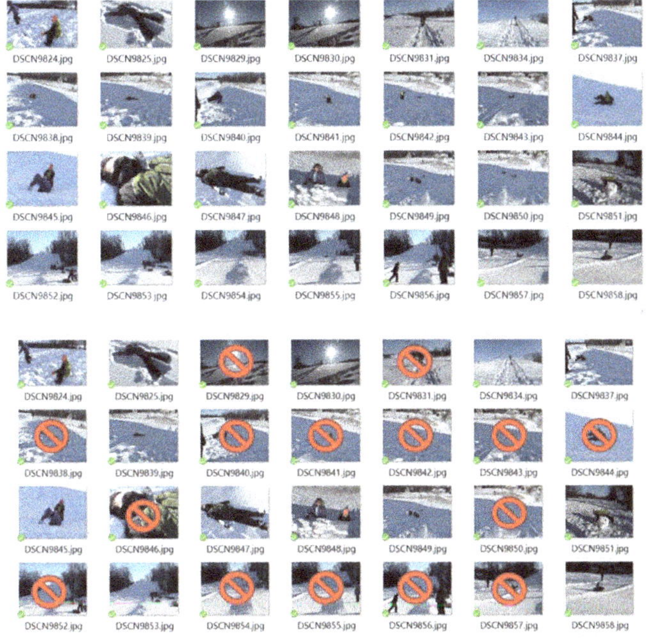

Before (above) and after (below) deciding which photos to keep.

3. **Events like birthday parties and family reunions**. Save eight to ten of the best photos from events. Many birthday parties occur year after year with a group of children and the photos tend to be repetitive and look the same. How many different angles of blowing out the candles on the cake do you need?

   Examples of photos you can toss: Unflattering angles of family members, all but one photo of the cake by itself, photos of people who are not relevant in your life anymore, any repetitive photos, just let them go!

   I recently helped a family organize over 10,000 printed photos from the 1980s and 1990s. They took a roll or two of film for each Christmas, Easter, and birthday party. With five children, the volume of photos was impressive. (24 to 48 pictures for two holidays and eight birthday gatherings each year). How many photos do you need of people opening presents? Just save the best few photos from each event and move on.

4. **Good quality photos**—Are your photos clear and in good condition? Save these photos if they meet the other conditions mentioned.

   Examples of photos you can toss: blurry photos, water-damaged photos, sticky photos—with the understanding that if the photo is important to you, save it.

Keeper Photo Examples

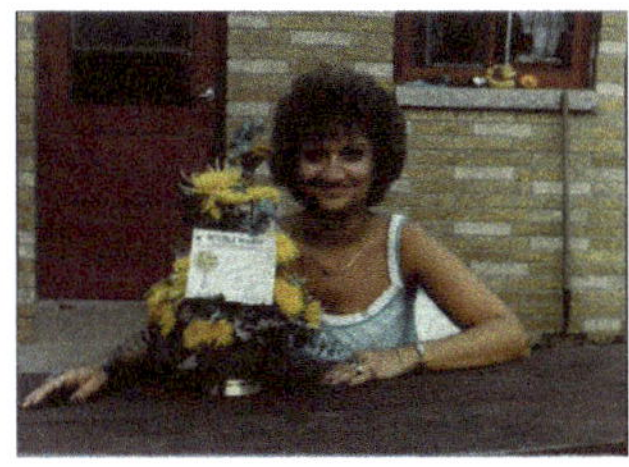

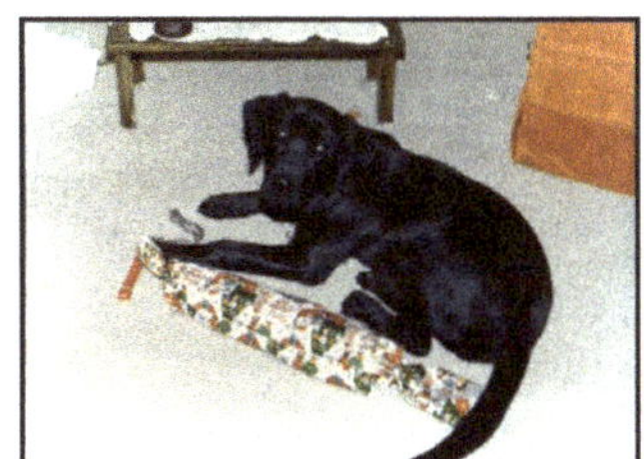

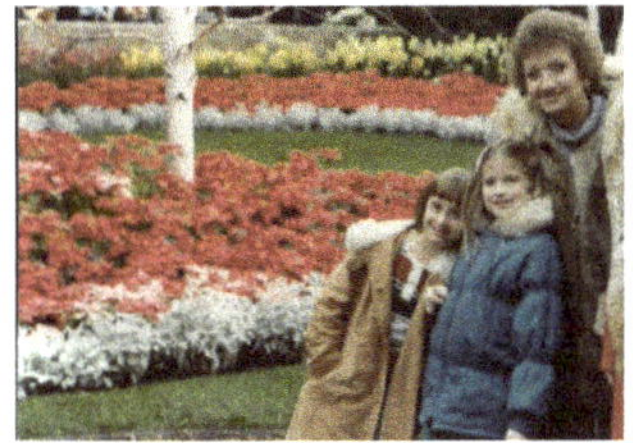

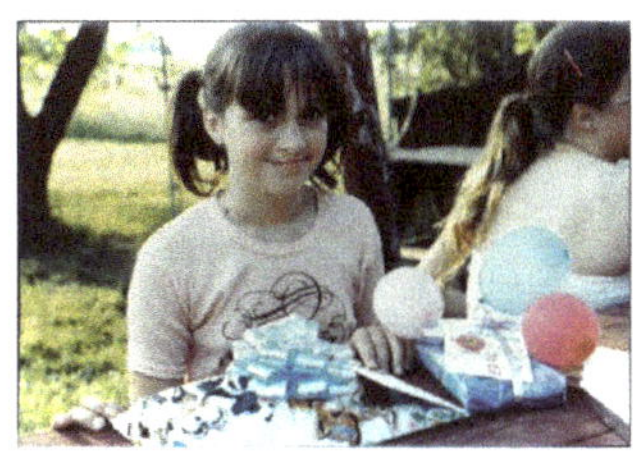

Non-Keeper Photo Examples

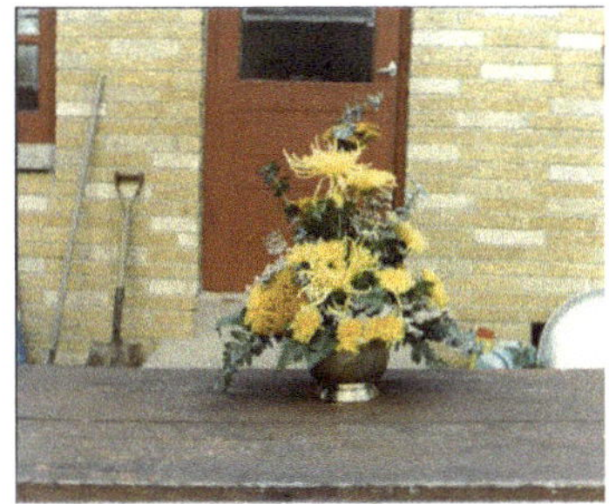

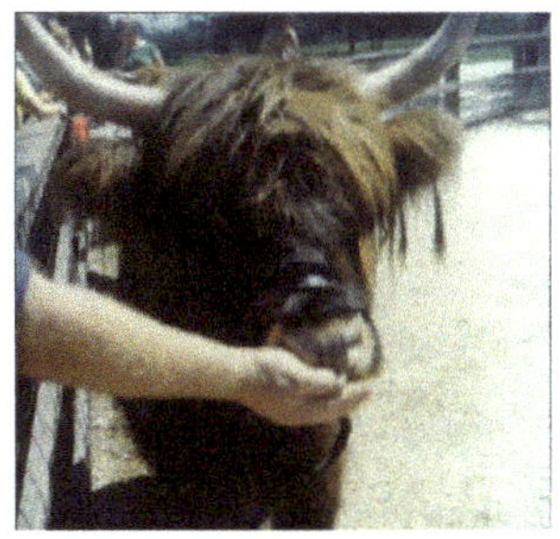

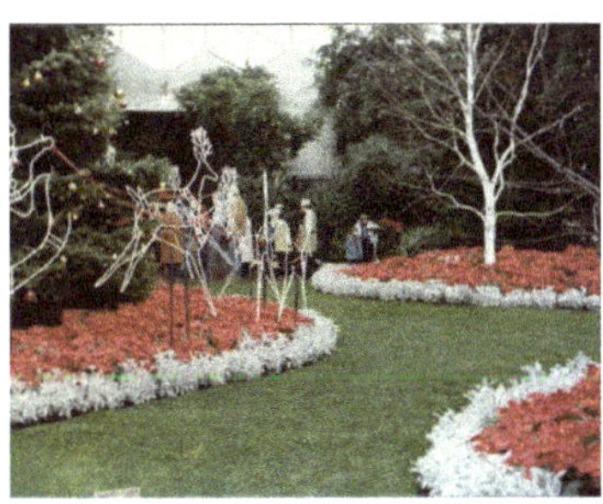

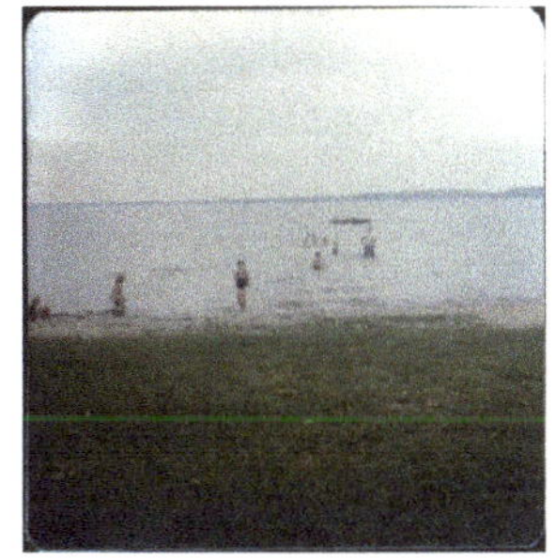

Hopefully, this chapter has given you some clues on which photos you can toss. The more photos you can weed out of your collection, the easier organizing will go.

The next step is learning how to organize your printed photo collection!

Remember: You don't need to save every photo. Keep the good ones that capture what life was like and what was important back then!

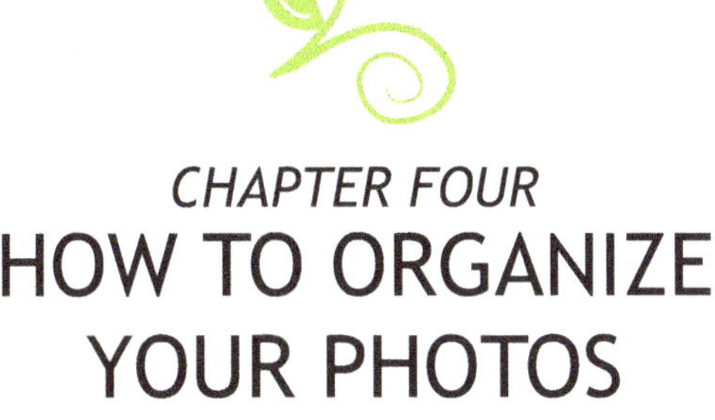

CHAPTER FOUR

HOW TO ORGANIZE YOUR PHOTOS

At Pixologie, we have used our photo organization system with clients since the beginning of our company. We have also taught our system to hundreds of people over the years and have received positive feedback.

Our system steps will be discussed in much more detail on the following pages, but I want you to see how the system works overall. Here's our simple system for organizing photos in a nutshell:

1. Bring all your photos to one place.
2. Sort all photos by major category.
3. Break down each major category's photos into subcategories
4. Final review

As you can see, you will be sorting through your photos in phases. It is possible you'll be handling your photos anywhere from two to four or more times, depending on your organizing style. Whenever possible, throw away photos that are duplicates, bad pictures, repetitive in nature, and so on. You will appreciate having less to sort in the final step of organization.

Once you have sorted and organized your photos into their final place, you will want to scan them, which is covered in Chapter Five.

Step One: Bring It All Together

Your first step is to collect all your photos in one place. Even if you are not starting right away, bringing all the photos together is a great beginning and a great feeling. Just start a table or a room and begin moving your boxes and albums there.

Let me remind you of all the places your photos may be hiding. From albums to boxes, envelopes, and baggies of photos, find as many as you can. Gather bins of photos, old framed photos in closets and school portraits. Look in any other place you have photos stashed. Do you have drawers full of photos? It's time to empty those out into one of the bins we mentioned in the tool section.

Why bring it all together?

- Seeing your photos all together helps provide perspective on what needs to be completed.
- Treating this project as an "all or nothing" venture provides you with a clear goal.
- Identifying and tossing duplicates become much easier.

- Enjoying the final organization is much more satisfying knowing you got it all!

Now, realistically, you will continue to find photos as you start your photo organization project and into the future. Add these to a "To Be Sorted" bin or section of your table for the time being as you collect them. At the onset, everything will need to be sorted, but as you progress, the "To Be Sorted" will grow smaller.

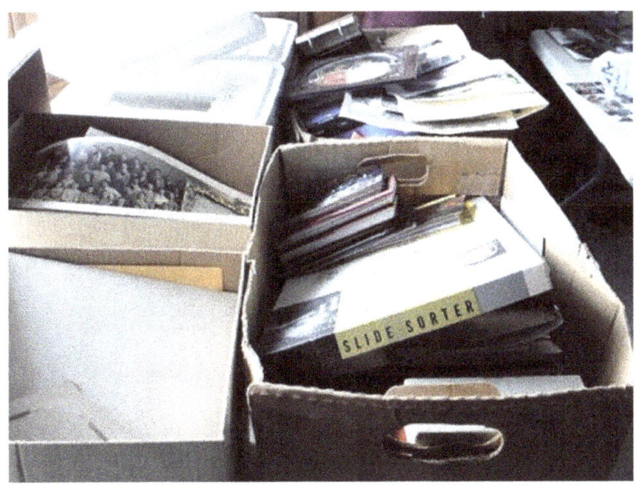

THE PHOTO ALBUM DILEMMA

If you have photos in albums, I bet you are wondering, "What's the plan for these?"

To "save" your photos for future generations, your photos must come out of the albums for scanning.

The decision as to whether or not to put the photos back into albums lies with you. Here are some questions to consider:

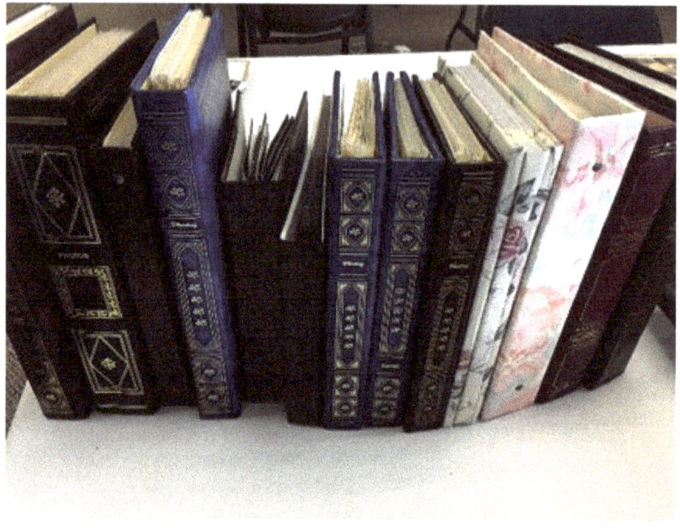

- Do I want to have these albums forever?
- Will my kids want these albums?
- Are my photos safe in them?
- Are these albums in good condition?
- Will I want or need to downsize my home someday?

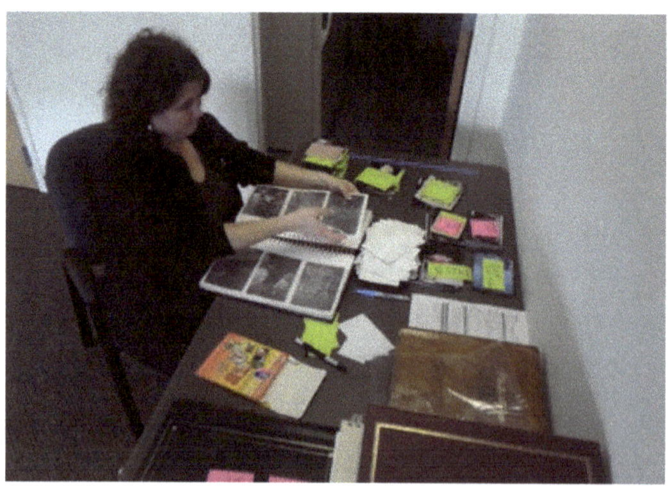

As you look through photo albums, do any photos stand out that you no longer need to save? Remember, back in the day; it was normal to save every photo taken because there were far fewer to look through.

I have seen people remove the photos from albums and throw away the deteriorating albums. In other cases, people intend to return their photos to their albums after organization and scanning. It is incredibly time-intensive to put pictures back into albums. Often, these intentions fail and so now, the person is storing both the empty albums and the stacks of photos. This situation creates a further mess in the future.

Also, returning pictures to unsafe photo albums defeats the entire purpose. Most albums from the 1980s and 1990s are not acid free and are damaging to the photos.

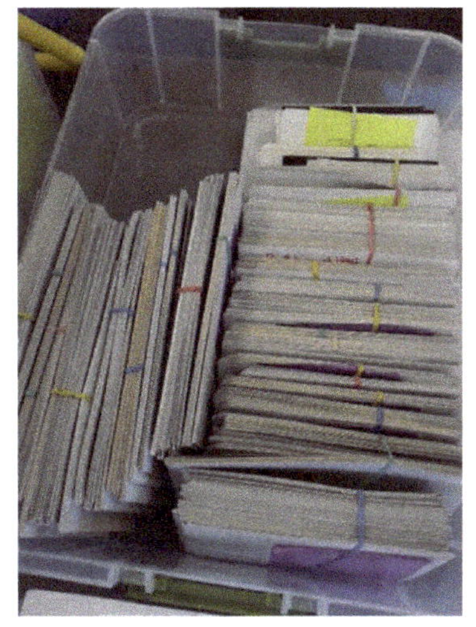

Here, these photos have been pulled from dated albums and secured with a rubber band. If you are interested in returning your photos to their albums, this system worked well for temporary storage and transport. I have also seen people put their photos in dated legal-sized envelopes for grouping to later return to albums.

You may decide to continue using photo albums. If so, you'll want to get rid of poor-quality photos and place the good pictures in new, photo-safe albums. Photo-safe albums will be free of acid, lignin, and PVC.

I'll be rooting for you either way whether you decide to keep or toss your photo albums—but I have found the most popular option is to purchase an elegant heirloom-quality, photo-safe box to store the photos after sorting.

Negatives and Slides

As you are bringing your photos together, you may find negatives and slides. We include these in our photo organization projects. We recommend setting negatives and slides aside to deal with separately after the printed photos.

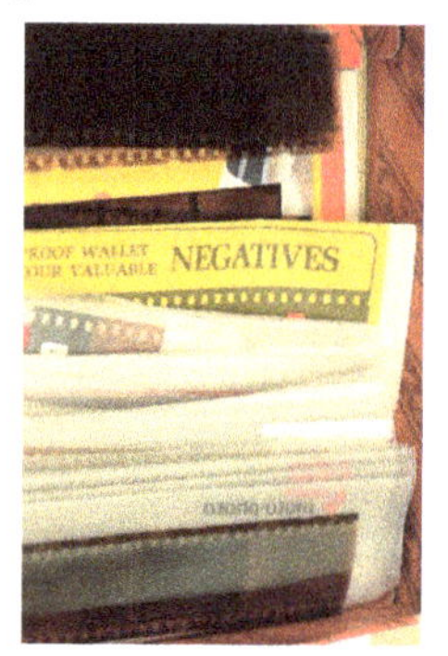

Negatives—Do you have negatives still stored in envelopes? You can toss them if you know for sure you have the photos already.

If the negatives are not with their photos and you are unsure if you have the photos, place the negatives in a bin and set to the side. Leave the negatives in their envelopes, along with any documentation, if possible.

It can be expensive to have reprints made or scan negatives (from 89 cents to $5 each). Try to figure out what might be missing in your photo collection before deciding to scan the negatives.

Slides—Well, there is good news and bad news about slides. Generally speaking, people in the 1960s, '70s and '80s did not have prints made of their slides. That's good news, so you don't have to worry about matching duplicate printed photos with their slides.

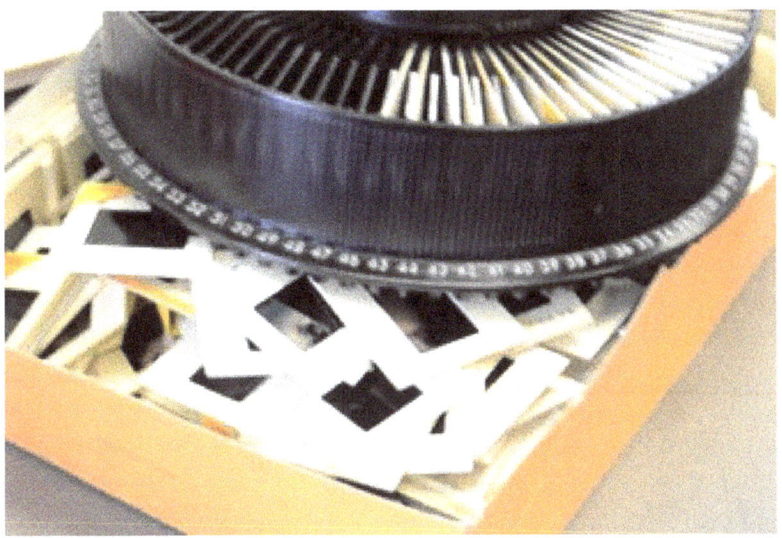

The bad news is that if you have slides, you may have hundreds of slides, maybe even thousands. Extremely popular in their time, slides offered families the ability to have photo shows in their living rooms.

As with negatives, scanning slides can be costly, depending on what type of service you use. If you have slides, set them aside for the time being. You can sort through them later and decide which ones to keep.

Once your printed photos have been organized, slides and negatives (if necessary) can be digitized as well.

Examples of People bringing All their photos together

Here are some photos of people bringing it all together! How do these photo collections compare with your current photo situation?

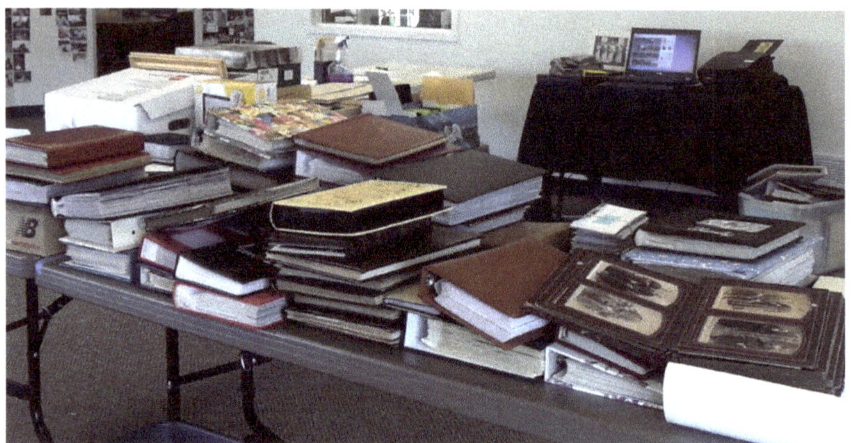

One client's collection: 55 photo albums and many other containers of photos.

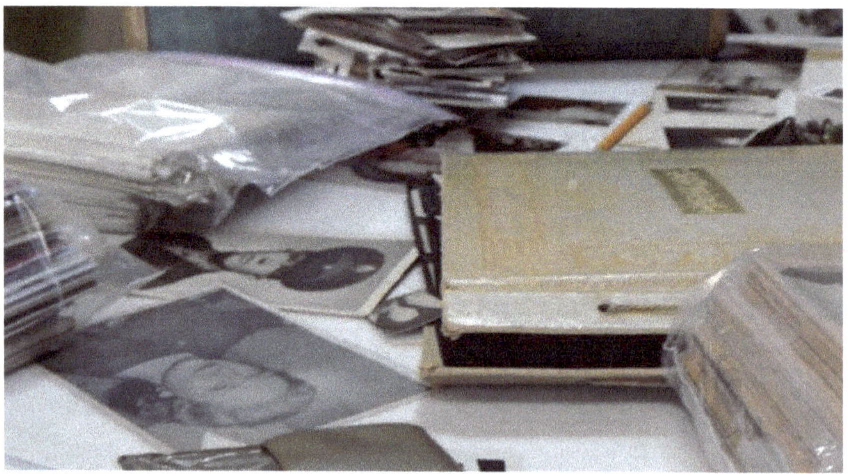

Sometimes people collect their photos and store them in suitcases.

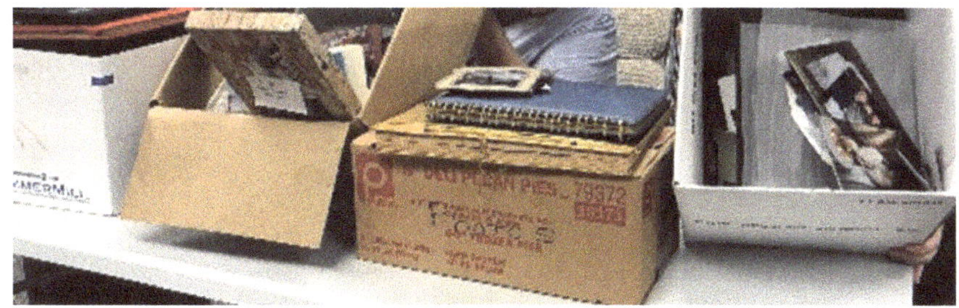

Here's another project where there are four large boxes of photos, a few albums and many loose photos. A great example of inherited photos being passed down. You'll learn more about this project later in the book.

Step Two: Organize by Major Category

If we organized our photos by all the separate events and moments in our lives, we would never finish. Our next step after bringing all the photos together is to organize the pictures by major category.

Choosing Your Photo Categories—This is the most important part of the project. You'll want to carefully consider what categories you'll use when organizing your photos. Halfway in, changing your mind will seriously dampen your enthusiasm in getting through those piles of pictures.

I recommend organizing photos chronologically for several reasons:

- Cross-referencing photos is easier when you have similar or duplicate photos to compare.
- You can refer to your Age Chart when not sure of a date and file your photo more accurately in a chronological system.

- When your photos are digitized, they can be labeled with the date and searched for by date.
- You can also use facial recognition software to efficiently tag people in pictures.

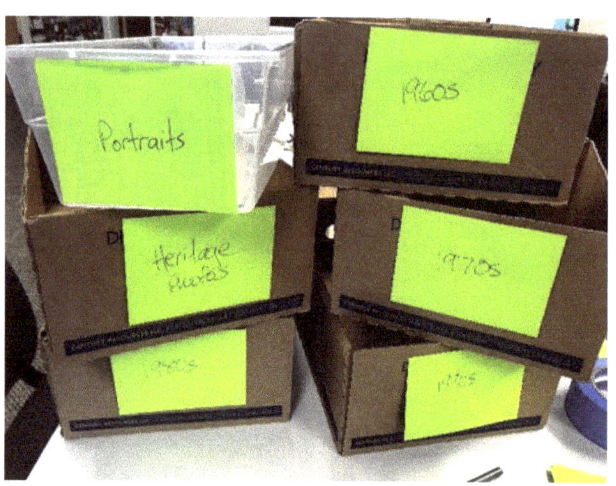

Example of major category bins.

It's okay if you want to organize photos by different method. I have seen successful photo organization projects when organized by person or other methods. Here are other major category types you might consider for sorting your photos:

- Subject (Family, Vacation, Sports, Events, Work, and others)
- Person (Mom, Dad, First Child, Second Child, etc.)
- Holiday (Valentine's Day, Easter, Fourth of July, Thanksgiving, Christmas and more)

- Album, box or source (Red Album, Alaska Album, Grandma's Box of Photos—essentially, naming the bin in which your photos were originally stored)
- Photo type, shape, and age (heritage photos, the 1930s & 1940s photos, square or rounded photos, etc.)

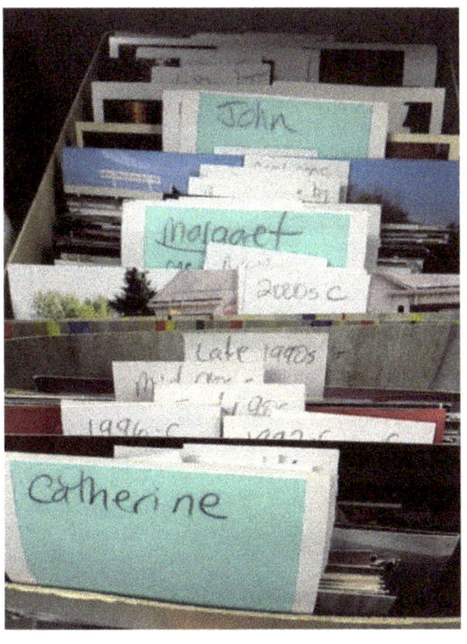

One of my clients, Mary, wanted to organize her photos by person despite my reservations. She explained she would be looking for her photos primarily by who was in the pictures. Her system worked well for her. It was great to see how fast she could work by sorting her pictures according to who was in the photo. In the end, we sorted her photos by person as the major category and then organized them by date for the subcategories. She was thrilled with the result.

A couple of observations about organizing photos by person:

- PROs—Mary can easily find photos of each one of her children. In fact, one daughter is getting married this fall, and she easily will be able to create a photo slideshow for the reception. (I scanned the photos and saved them into digital folders organized by person as well.)

- CONs—Photos from special family events will be split across four to five different categories depending upon who is in the photo. If you want all the photos from one of your family events, you would have to search through each person's photos to find those pictures.

Do you have a large number of inherited photos from your parents, grandparents, or another family member? It is appropriate to set those aside from your own family photo collection as a separate project.

It is up you to determine how you can best organize your photo collection. The accomplishment will still feel as great when your photos are sorted, no matter what categories you used to sort them!

Exceptions to Your Categories

Portraits—If you are like many other people, your portrait photos will be scattered all over the place. You'll find many duplicates and different sizes. Keep portraits in a separate bin for easier sorting at a later time in your project. Once ALL your portrait photos have been located throughout your house, then sort by person. If you like, you can organize them by date as well. It's just a quick tip that has helped us save time.

OPTIONAL—Separate your immediate family member school portraits from the portraits you received from your extended

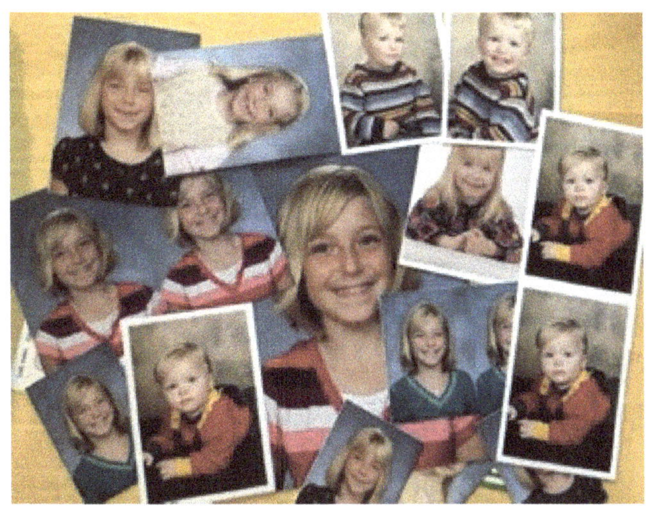

family and friends. Some of these from outside your family may be okay to throw away or return to the person who gave it to you.

Photos of Other People You Don't Want Anymore—Most of my clients set aside photos of others to give to those people who are in the pictures. If you are going to do this, create a bin labeled something like "Give to Someone Else" and put all the photos that you want to give away in that bin.

Christmas Photo Cards—It is truly hard to throw any photo away. That is why I see so many Christmas photo cards in people's collections. If you can't yet toss these old cards of other people's families, then set them in their own bin for sorting. (*Secret: I am one of those people who can't do it!*)

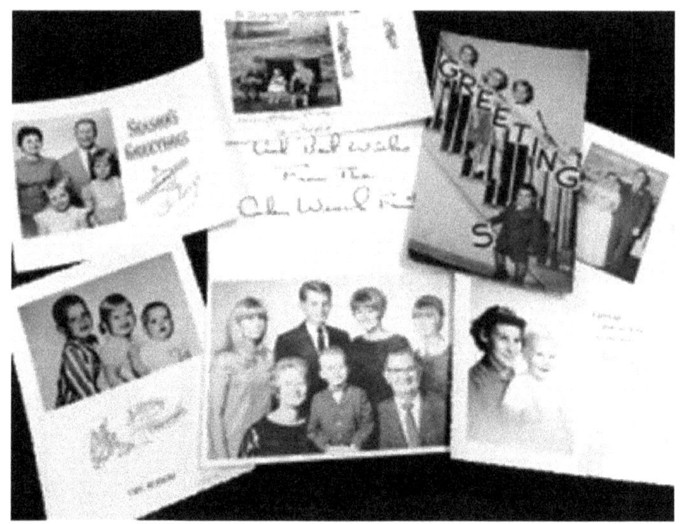

Holiday cards from the 1960s.

Memorabilia—As you go through your photos, you will likely find memorabilia (class certificates, letters, cards, yearbooks, event programs, artwork, and much more. Don't get caught up in these materials; set them in their own box for another time. These are not part of your photo organization project. Later on, you may return to the box to organize the items by person and those items can be also be scanned for preservation.

Example of Major Categories

Here's a list of the major categories created by one of my clients (you'll see photos on upcoming pages):

- Heritage photos (Mom's side)
- Heritage photos (Dad's side)
- 1950s
- 1960s

- 1970s
- 1980s
- 1990s
- 2000s
- 2010s
- Portraits
- Career Photos
- Photos to give away

System for Organizing Photos by Major Category

Choose your categories and label your bins for placing the corresponding photos. Create bins for the categories as you go along.

1. Pick a section, an album, box, or envelope of photos to start organizing into the bins. OPTIONAL – use index cards to group photos. But don't let it slow you down.
2. Sort those photos into the corresponding bin categories, DISCARDING the bad photos, duplicates, etc. right away. (Remember, don't reminisce!). Throwing away photos now means that you won't have to look at them and decide again later.
3. Complete that set of photos and move on to a new batch of photos to organize.
4. Repeat the steps until all your photos have been sorted into a major category.
5. Don't forget to keep tossing photos.

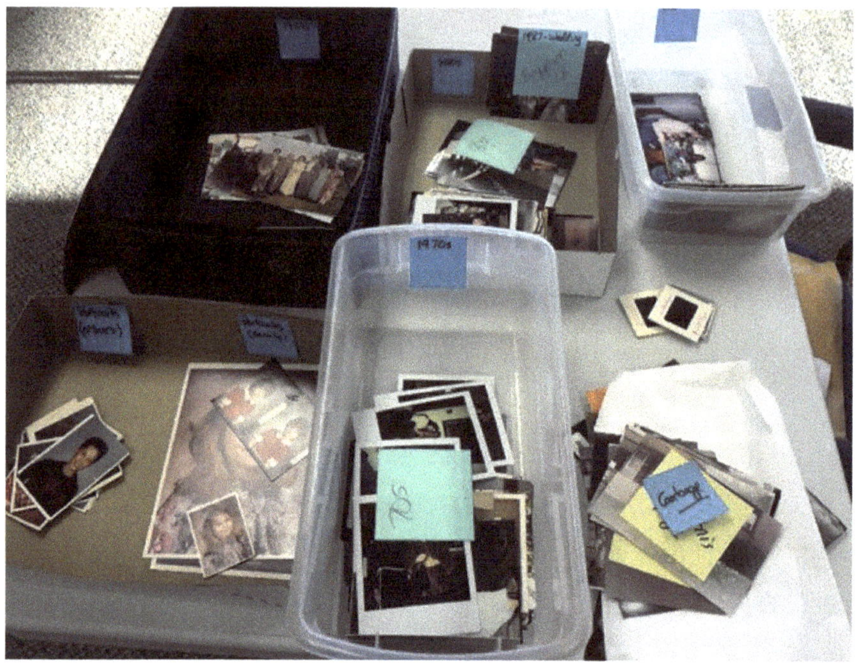

Here's a simple set of bins. Back row – 1980s, 1990s, 2000s. Front row – Portraits, 1970s, Garbage. With a few slides found in the mix from one drawer of photos.

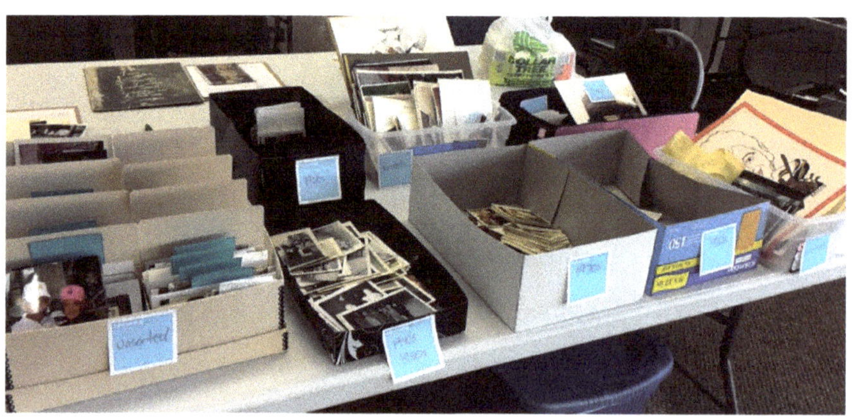

And here's another large example of bins by decade.
You can see a memorabilia bin at the right end.

EXAMPLE: CHRONOLOGICAL PHOTO ORGANIZING

The following photos are from one client who probably had more than 20,000 printed photos to organize. We started organizing by decade.

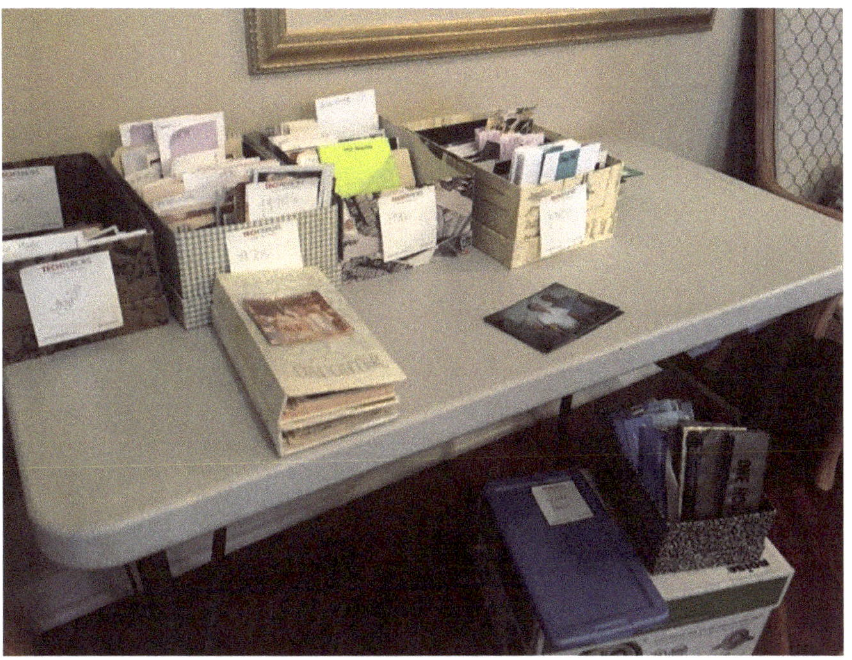

The boxes from left to right read 1960s, 1970s, 1980s, and 1988.

1988 had so many photos already separated, we just added a box to hold those particular photos. You can also see some index cards and sticky notes where I separated years that were obvious (because they came out of neatly organized albums that the client discarded after removing the photos.)

The albums in front of the 1970s are from the 1970s but have individual notes with each photo and we haven't decided how to proceed with those. We set the albums with the other '70s pictures for the time being. Below the table is a photo box that holds negatives and an office paper box filled with more envelopes of negatives. We will look through those once we get through organizing the majority of her photos.

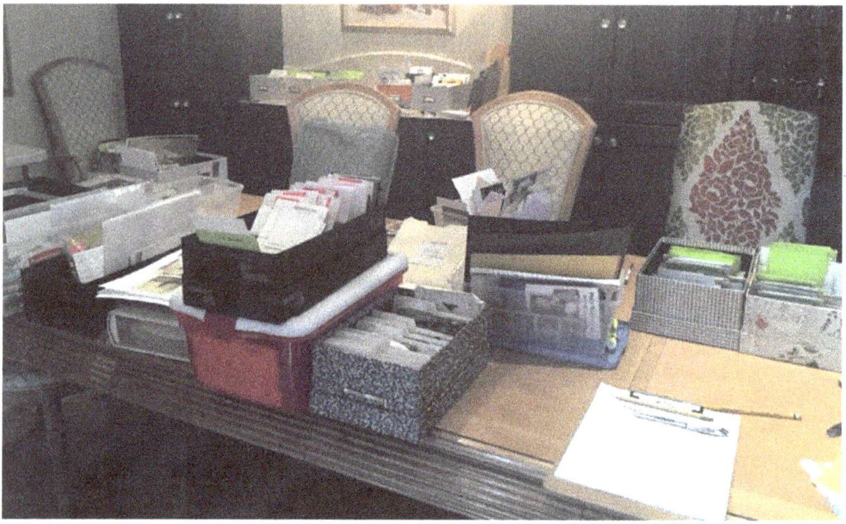

In this photo, you can see my client's other bins of photos on her table and the back shelf of her dining room. Each time I visit we tackle another box or two of photos to sort.

There were also two large bins of gallon-sized Ziploc bags of photos underneath her table with close to 5,000 photos labeled by year, which was extremely helpful.

Example: Photos Organized by Person

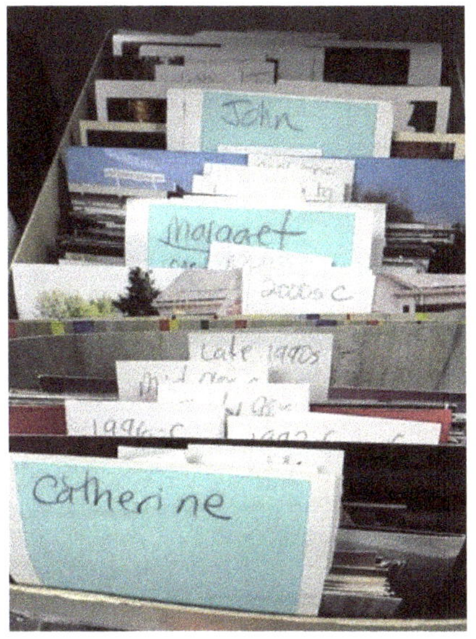

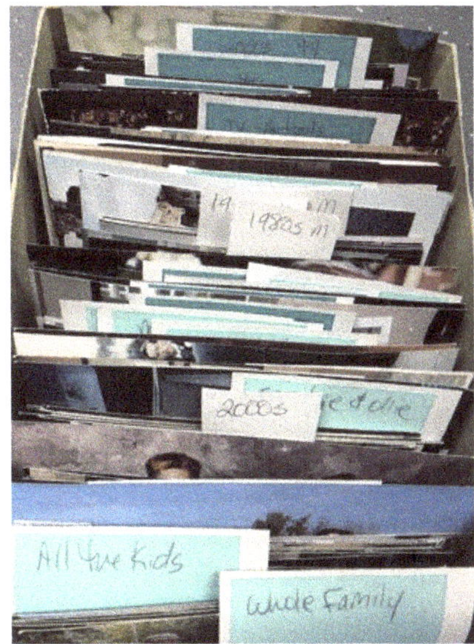

In the photos above, you can see Mary's boxes of photos sorted by person and already organized by her subcategories. During Step Two, there were no subcategory index tabs with dates on them. We sorted each child's photo by date for the subcategory. All the photos were disorganized and had to be sorted extensively.

You are looking at Mary's final organization here. Mary finished her organization fast due to her ability to quickly look at a photo, toss it if necessary, and move on to the next picture.

I can't tell you how long Step Two—Organize by Major Category—will take because it depends entirely on you! Will you be a "Super-Sorter" and zoom through your photos, tossing the duplicates, bad photos, and repetitive photos quickly and decisively? I have seen clients finish their initial sorting into categories in a weekend. Others have taken a lot longer.

There is no award for the best organizing or fastest job! The goal is to simply finish Step Two. Don't quit!

Step Three: Break Down Major Categories

Okay, we've reviewed sorting your photos into their major categories. Now we can fine tune each major category into subcategories. As you go through these photos for the second time, continue to toss photos as you can. At this point, you should start remembering photos and getting a sense of what duplicates you come across.

Chronological Category Breakdown—If you sorted your photos by decades to start with, now is the time to separate the decades into years where possible.

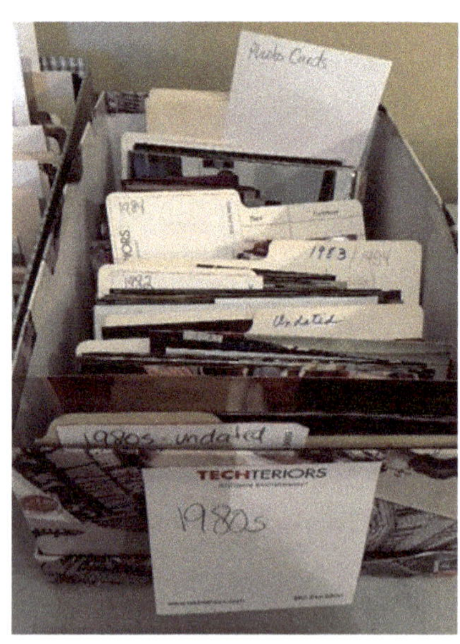

In this photo, you can see we have started dividing up the 1980s photos into years. Note that we have several index cards with an "undated" label. We may never figure out those dates more precisely than the decade.

Also note in the back an index card labeled "Photo Cards." These are similar to the category of "Portraits" and I'd recommend separating them from your photo collection as well. The original photo you used on the card SHOULD stay in your photo collection. Some clients like to have their holiday photo cards stored together in order.

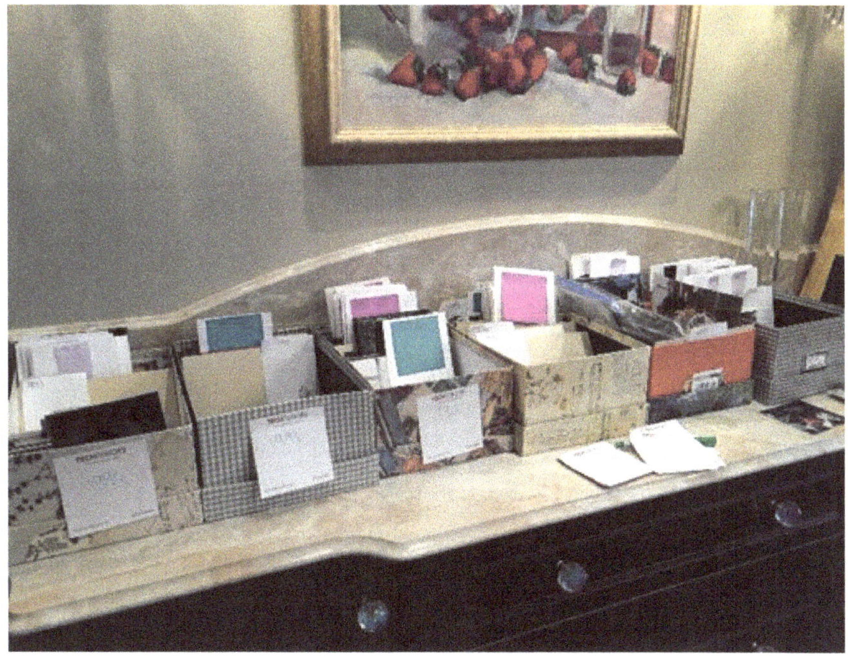

The 1990s photos were broken down by year in this photo. Remember the Ziplock bags of photos under our client's table? Each Ziplock bag was labeled with the year the photos were taken. So, our next step was to incorporate those bags of photos into the photos we had organized from other places earlier in our process.

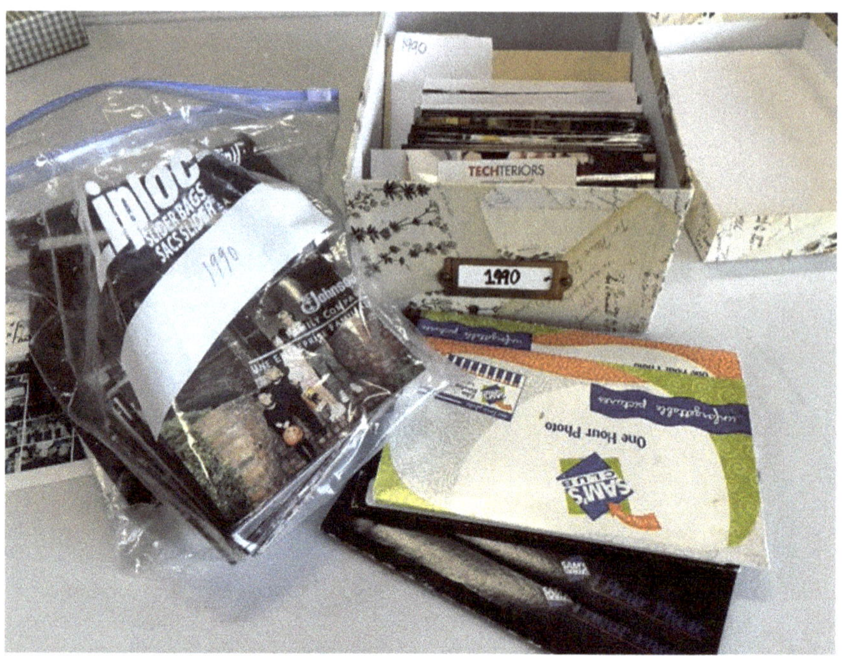

You can see the two bags and box are labeled 1990. They need to be consolidated, de-duplicated, and the envelopes tossed.

TIP: If you are sorting, use index cards to transfer the information on the envelopes (if any). This way you can toss the photo envelopes, which are a hindrance to viewing photos in your boxes and take up space.

Further Chronological Category Breakdown—Some people find that sorting by year provides a great level of organization, and they are content to stop the sorting at this point. I like to go one step further and organize by month within the years. This helps in the 1980s and 1990s, because duplicates were so prevalent then.

So, once you have sorted your photos from decades into years, the next step is to sort each year by months. This part may seem tedious. It is the final step in organizing your photos and you don't need to do it. However, sorting by month can provide a high level of accuracy by date and assist with duplicate removal. Also, it's nice for your holiday photos to be in order. For example, holiday photos should be at the end of the year instead of mixed in with other photos throughout the year.

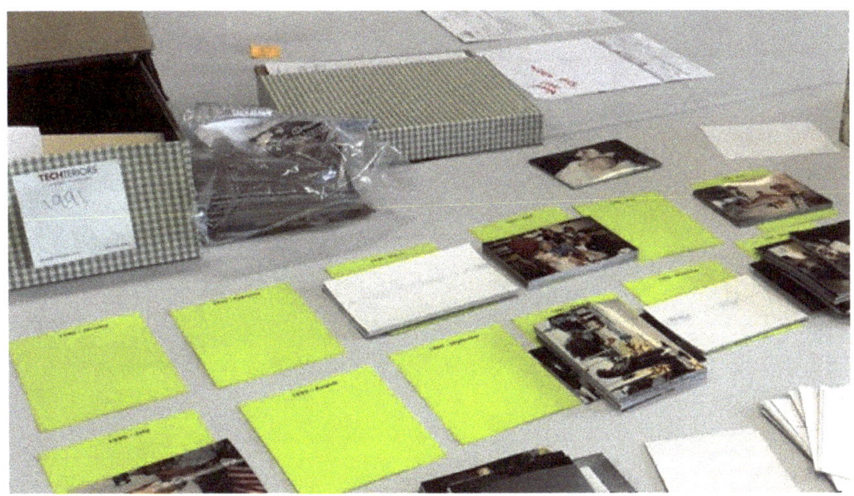

Each of the index cards is labeled with the months of 1990 (1990 – January; 1990 – February 1990, etc.).

I also have included an index card labeled 1990-Undated for photos of indeterminate month. Then I started sorting the photos by month. Context clues (Easter, Halloween, etc.) and markings on the back made sorting fairly easy. When dealing with a year's worth of photos for the first time, it is easier to

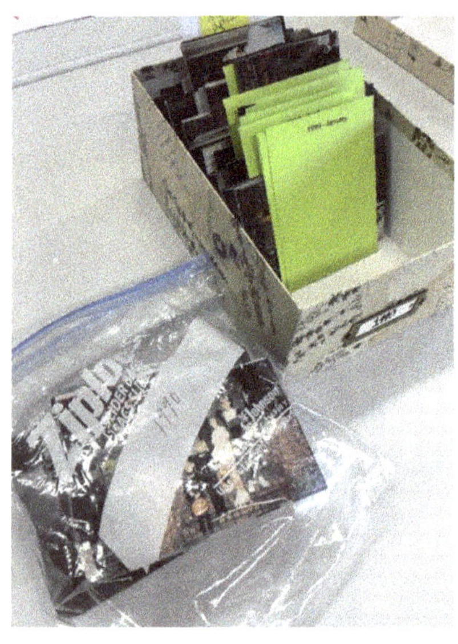

sort them onto a flat surface before moving stacks into the box.

I stacked the organized photos in the photo box by the months in 1990. In the back, the last index card includes the undated photos. My client will review these on our next visit, and she will attempt to put them in the months they belong if possible.

Also note, I realized that I hadn't sorted the photos from the second Ziploc bag. Fortunately, it was easy to sort these photos with the others because I recognized some of the events.

Example of Step Three: Sorting Chronologically by Subcategory

Remember my client's table of bins labeled by decade? We have made significant progress here.

Once you have sorted your photos chronologically down to the month where possible, it is easier to add the random photos in your "To Be Sorted" bin. It's great to grab a photo, go to the month, and find other photos from the same event.

Would You Like a Set of these Index Cards?

FREE DOWNLOAD – INDEX CARD TEMPLATE Word Document with these index cards labeled by year and month. Find it at www.pixologieinc.com under Tools. Simply print on your favorite color of paper and cut in four.

ORDER A SET – at www.pixologieinc.com/shop

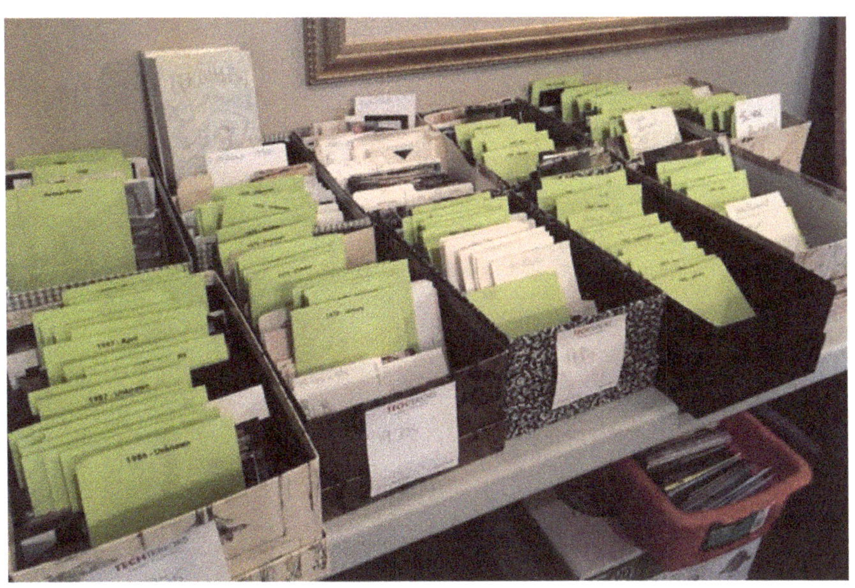

Other Category Types Broken Down into Subcategories

You will find many different options of how to break down the other types of categories. As you go through your photos, no doubt other subcategories will come to light. Here are some ideas for you.

SORTING BY SUBJECT: Major Categories/Subcategories

- Family – Grandparents, parents, children, pets
- Vacation – Locations, types of vacations (cruise, in-state, European), Who you traveled with
- Sports – Children's activities, school sports
- Events – Holidays (breakdown to individual holidays) reunions, weddings, birthday parties, faith events
- Work – Co-workers, work events, awards and recognition

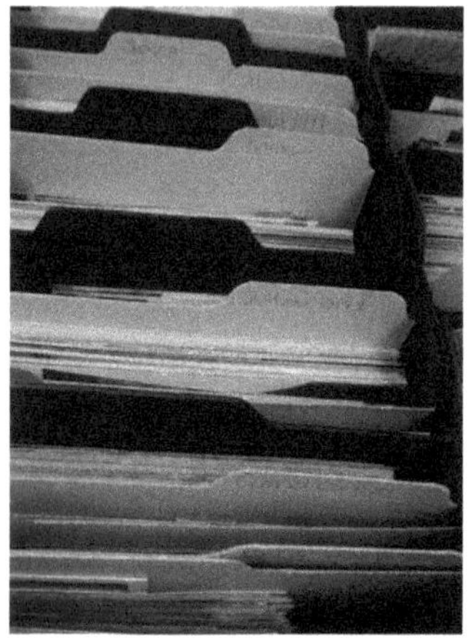

The photo to the left shows the photo box with vacation pictures, sorted by the places where the couple had traveled.

SORTING BY PERSON: Major Categories/Subcategories

- Self – (you can organize these photos by date, or you can break them down by different categories as well.) Ideas include: growing up, dating years, marriage, raising children, life without children, travel, etc.)
- Spouse
- Parents
- Child (individual children, group photos of children; hobbies, etc.)
- Extended family (sort by family groups)
- Family friends
- Specific family activities that are traditions (camping, waterskiing, sporting events)

These categories and subcategories are interchangeable. You don't have to be completely bound by one method or the other. For instance, as a rule, I sort my photos chronologically.

However, last year, I collected a bunch of photos of my aunt from various places to create a photo poster board for her birthday. I don't store these chronologically because I don't know the date taken, and they are not part of any event my family attended. However, I have stored them in a folder labeled with her name in case I need them in the future.

You can sort chronologically and have a separate container of photos for special pictures. One of my clients pulled out baptism photos because her children were at the stage of having babies. She wanted to easily share the baptism photos.

SORTING PORTRAITS AND HOLIDAY PHOTO CARDS

Let's expand a little bit more on sorting portraits and photo cards.

Portraits: Subcategories include: Immediate Family, Extended Family and Friends). Then sort by person and after that, by year, tossing the duplicates, which may be plentiful. I never felt right about throwing away the extra portraits of my children, but there comes a time when it is okay to let go of those dinky wallet-sized extras!

Holiday Photo Cards: Subcategories include: Family, Extended Family and Friends. Then sort by year. As for your own family Christmas photo cards? You don't have to save the 25 extra cards you never sent, just save a couple and keep them all in one place in your photo collection.

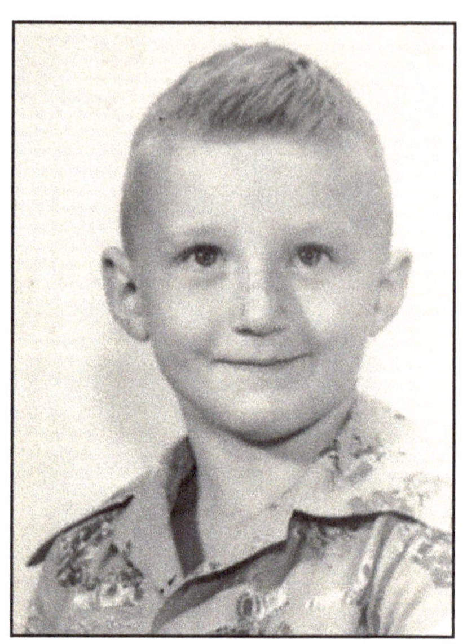

Question—Here's a school portrait of my dad from 1952. Would I sort this into portraits or my heritage photos?

Answer—Good question. I tend to put all photos of my parents into a bin categorized as "Heritage Photos," even the portraits. And I would apply that rule of thumb to all those ancestor-type photos I may come across.

SPECIFIC STEPS TO BREAK DOWN INTO SUBCATEGORIES:

1. Take one major category bin and separate photos into the subcategories you have identified.
2. Label and use index cards to separate the subcategories.
3. Eliminate doubles and bad photos where possible.
4. Repeat until all major categories have been sorted into subcategories.
5. If desired, further sort subcategories.

Step Four: Final Review

Okay, you have finally sorted and combed through your photos at least two times, if not more. Do you feel like your photo collection is set for the scanning process? We like to have people go through their photos one last time to weed out any final unwanted photos.

Remember our client with the 55 photo albums and numerous other containers? We estimate that we started with 13,000 photos to organize.

After Steps Two and Three, we had narrowed down the photo collection to around 10,000 photos. During the final review, we eliminated another thousand photos. This stack of archival legacy boxes went from five down to four.

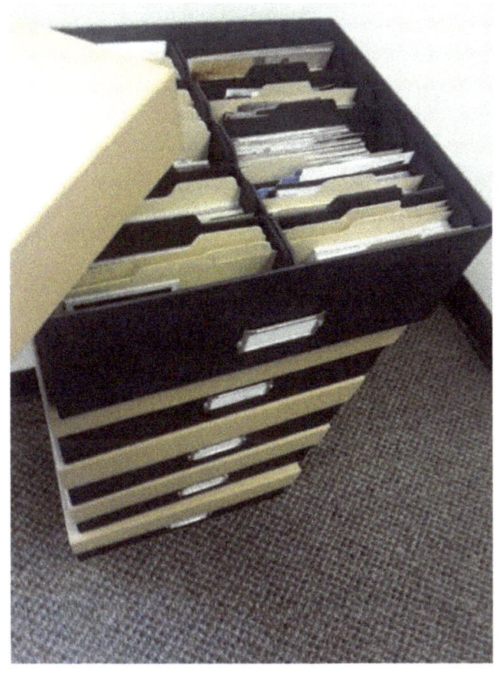

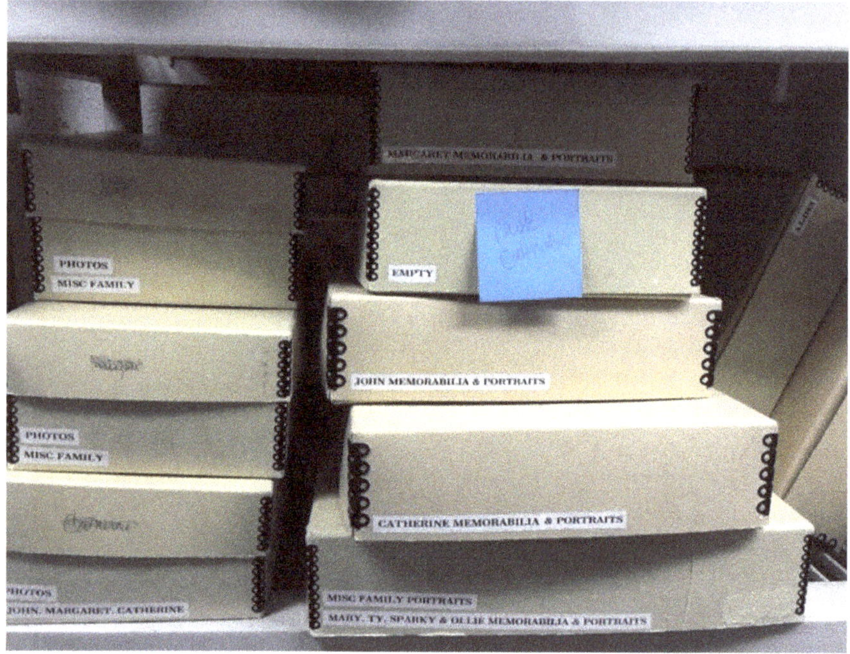

Above, another example of completed organization. The bin with the "empty" label is filled with the family's photo calendars and is just waiting for a printed label.

Remember: Your photo organization journey does not end when your photos are sorted and stored neatly. You need to back up your photos digitally to ensure your memories are preserved and protected. This leads into our next chapter: ***How To Save Your Photos.***

Special Note: Slides and Negatives

Remember, we set aside the slides and negatives. Now that you are a photo organizing pro, you can sort through your slides. You can use a light box to sort and keep the best of the slides. The light box may also help with determining if you need to save any of your negatives.

We use an old-fashioned light box for sorting slides and a Wolverine slide and negative scanner for a low-cost, do-it-yourself solution. If you want higher quality images, you'll need to consider professional scanning.

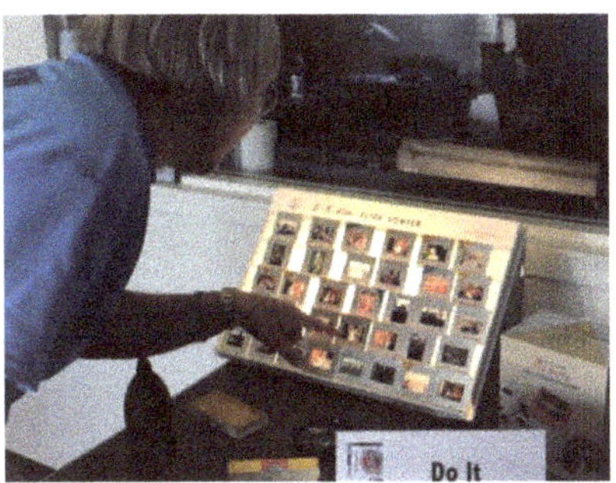

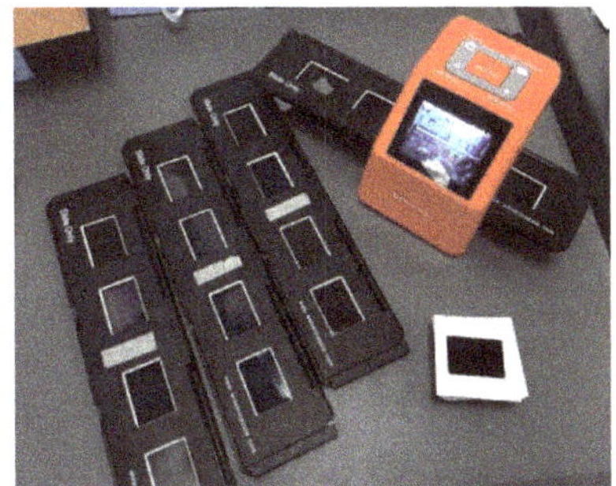

Heritage Photos

Let's expand on the Heritage Photos major category in case you come across some older photos. Remember to handle these carefully, especially if they are fragile. I consider heritage photos to be those old photographs dating from the 1800s to the 1930s or 1940s.

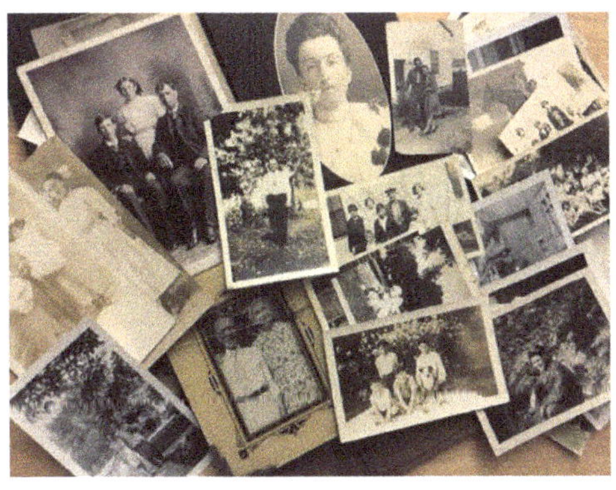

When you have gathered all your photos in one place and can actually see all the heritage photos together, you might be surprised.

- There are often many duplicates (especially of portraits, but of regular photographs also.)
- There are often repetitive photos!
- There are clues to help identify who's who (i.e., a note on one copy of a photo provides a name for a person who appears in other photos, and so on.)

These are ambrotypes from the late 1800s. Our client's ancestor's names were etched on the side of the case!

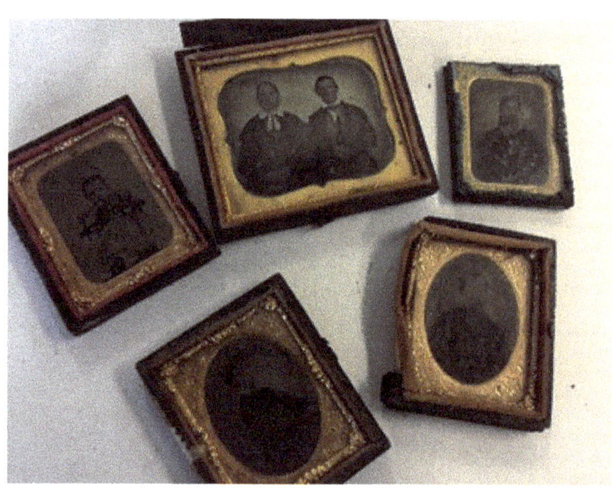

FREE DOWNLOAD: Identifying Ambrotypes, Daguerreotypes & Tintypes is available at www.pixologieinc.com under Pixologist Tools.

Lastly, if you are unable to identify the people in the photo and you have no family members to help, it may be time to let go of those photos.

Another suggestion is to donate unidentified old photos to your local historical society or upload to genealogical websites. See the Resource Section at the back of the book for a few of these websites.

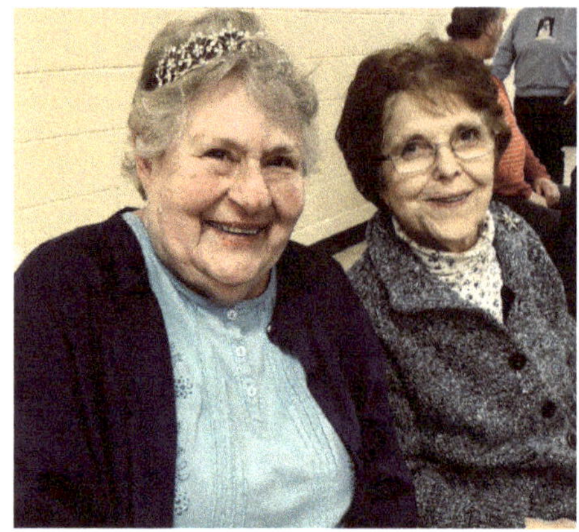

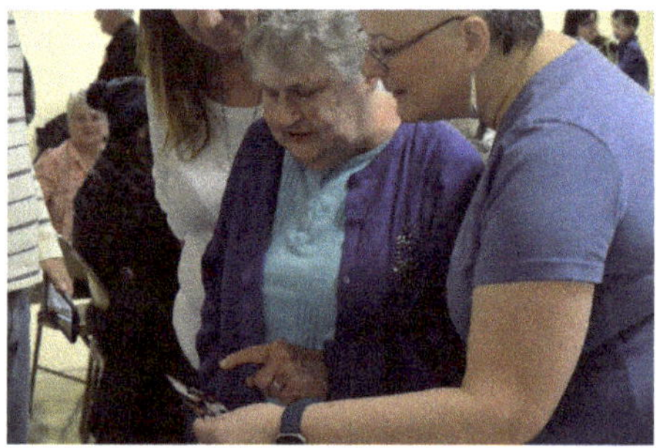

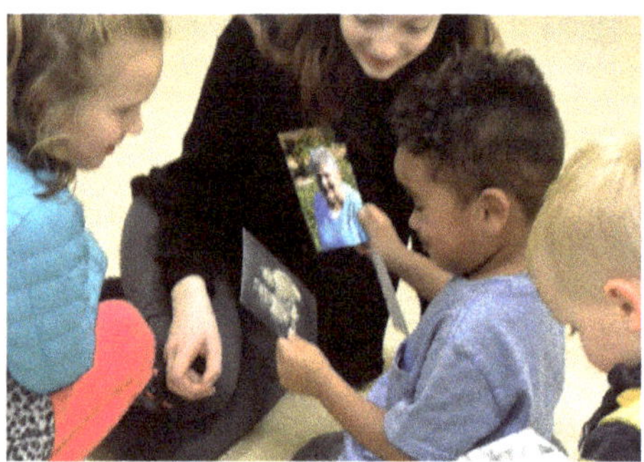

When photos are organized, its easy to pull them for a special milestone birthday party. Marie's 80th birthday party featured family photos from when she was little. Marie is Pixologie Co-Founder Ann Matuszak's mother and holds a very special place in our heart. See Marie's great-grandson looking at pictures of her when she was young. Yes, photos connect generations!

CHAPTER FIVE

HOW TO SAVE YOUR PHOTOS

Now that your photos are sorted and organized, it's time to save your photos. Let's define what "save" means. Within the scope of this book, I consider a photo saved when it meets both of these conditions:

1. It is stored in an organized fashion, and you can find the photo when you need or want it. We've shown you how to do this.
2. It is backed up in two other places—a location within your home and a location outside of your home such as a family member's home, a safe deposit box or the cloud.

If either of these conditions is not met, your photos are in danger of being lost to time, disaster, or other unfortunate situation.

NUMBER 1: STORED IN AN ORGANIZED FASHION

If Number One is not met, situations will arise when you are looking for certain photos, and you cannot find the pictures. These situations often take place around major family events when sharing photos and memories matters the most. We've had clients with the following situations:

- ***Funeral of a parent***—Family members must rush around to find photos of their mother or father for the funeral home. Some of the photos are on copy paper from an ink-jet printer. No one knows where the originals are, and the photos are poor in quality.

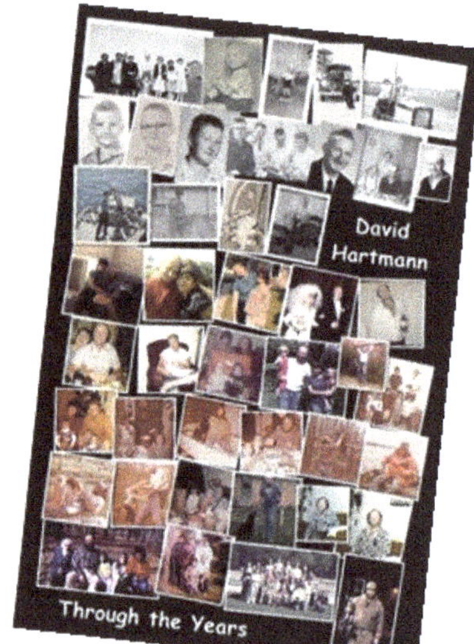

- ***Celebration of a wedding anniversary***—A daughter must take a photo of a picture in a frame to include that special memory in a photo slideshow.
- ***High school graduation***—We've had several clients with children graduating from high school or college who must scramble at the last minute to put together photo boards.

It's interesting to see how many of my clients have envelopes of photos from different events over the years, which add to their photo chaos. Invariably, when photos are pulled out for such events, the pictures are not returned to their proper place.

Does this sound familiar? For those of you who have already organized your photos, did you have envelopes of certain family members that had been used for a special event?

NUMBER 2: BACKED UP IN TWO OTHER PLACES

If your photos are not backed up in two other places, your photos could be lost to fire, floods, theft, and other types of damage. I've seen the following:

- A basement flood soaks wedding photos thought to be stored in a water-tight container.
- A fire destroys a home and all its contents. The family must rely on relatives to provide copies of pictures.
- A smartphone is stolen, with hundreds of special holiday photos gone forever.
- A box of photos is lost during a move.

Throughout this book, I have talked about organizing printed photos. It is not realistic to have two printed copies of your photo collection. When considering how to back up your photos in two places, I am now referring to creating a digital copy of your printed photos.

Digital copies are created by scanning your entire printed photo collection. Once you have the digital copies, you can easily store the copies in two locations, one inside the house and one off-site. I'll discuss this more after diving into scanning.

Scanning Your Photos

More than twenty years ago, the first scanners became available. I remember my dad's first flatbed scanner purchase, which was well over $1,000. We were so excited about the ability to scan photos and other documents.

Flash forward to the present—I find most households have the potential to scan pictures with their printers. However, the majority of people I meet don't scan their photos because they don't know how or they find the process too slow.

Fortunately, technology has come a long way, and faster scanners are available now. When you scan a photo, you want to end up with a digital file that is a JPG (most everyone) or a TIFF (advanced users). Please see Appendix B for recommended scanning settings.

Also, for those who are interested, once your photo has been scanned, you can add metadata to the digital file. Metadata includes the original date taken, tagging, comments, and more.

Here's a quick overview of the different scanning options available:

PORTABLE SCANNERS

From wand-type scanners to the Flip-Pal Mobile scanner, these options offer simplicity and convenience for scanning photos. You don't need a computer to scan photos with these devices. For the most part, scanners like these cost below $200.

With wand-type scanners, you simply feed the photos through the slot. The digital images are captured on a camera SD card. You can then transfer the photos from your card to your computer. Typically, wand scanners do need a power supply.

The Flip-Pal Mobile scanner allows you to scan photos wherever you are. While it only fits 4x6-inch photos, the Flip-Pal comes with software to "stitch" scanned sections of a larger photograph together. The Flip-Pal has a small screen so you can see your photo as it is scanned.

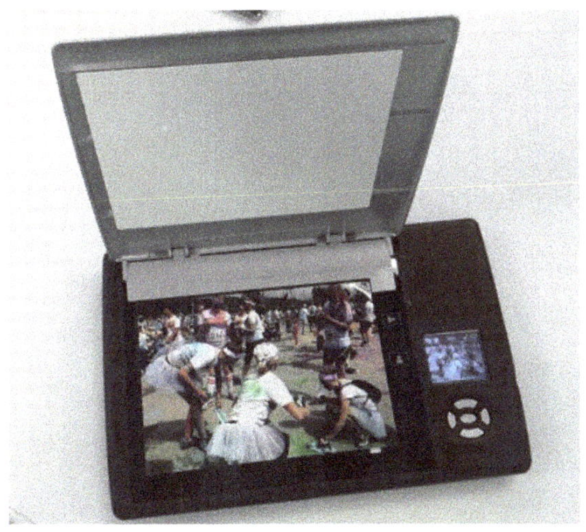

Flip-Pal Mobile scanner.

PRINTER SCANNERS

Yes, you can scan photos with your printer/scanner in a pinch. However, we recommend this method of scanning only when it is necessary. Around ten years ago, I had to scan around 400 photos for a family member's funeral with a printer scanner. It didn't cost me anything, but the job took over six hours to complete—and it was frustrating. Using your printer to scan a large number of photos takes a very long time.

Typically, your printer scanner comes with software that allows you to save your scans in a folder on your computer. Be sure to save as a JPG and not a PDF and with a resolution of 300 or 600 DPI.

FLATBED PHOTO SCANNERS

Early on in helping people with their photos, we relied on our flatbed photo scanner. Coming with their own photo scanning software, these scanners allow you to scan multiple pictures at the same time. Then, each picture is saved separately as a JPG.

Also, you will find there are more options in how you save photos to your computer and how you name your files. But

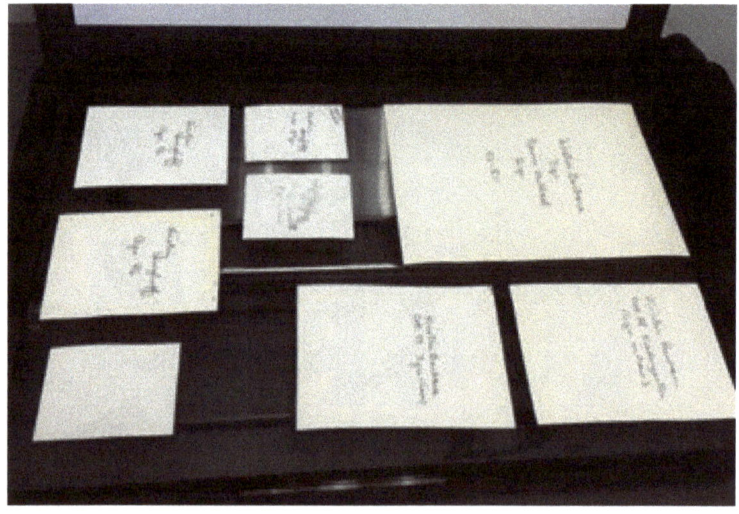

This flatbed scanner saved each photo separately.

these scanners also are time consuming to use. If you are dealing with fragile old photos, however, you must use a flatbed scanner.

HIGH-SPEED PHOTO SCANNERS

When you have more than a few hundred photos to scan, a high-speed photo scanner will make life very easy for you. We use the Kodak Alaris Picture-Saver Scanning System (Kodak Alaris PS80), which scans up to 85 photos a minute! Yes, the Kodak Alaris PS80 scans at an unbelievable speed. The PS80 scans faster than we can keep up with it.

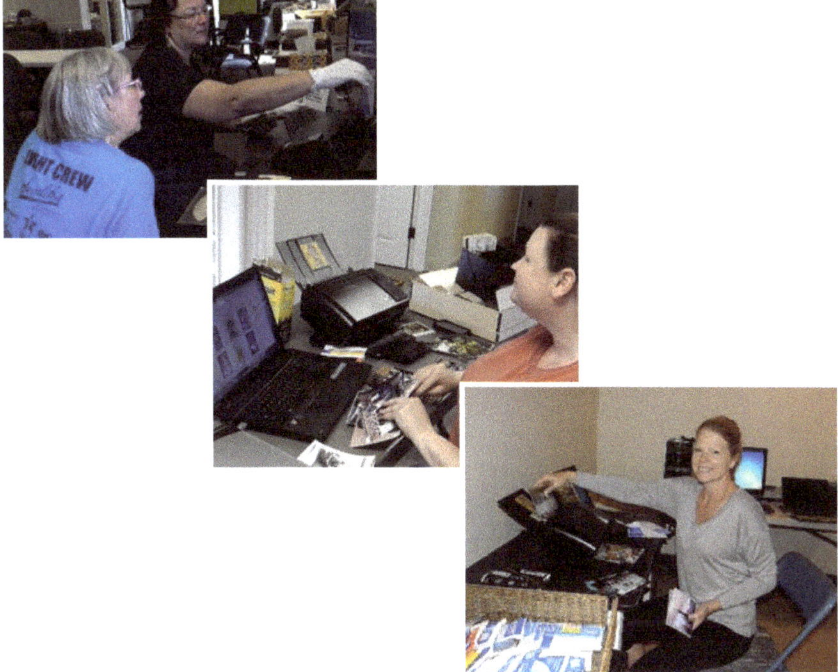

Alaris Picture-Saver Scanning Systems start around $1500, which is cost-prohibitive for many people. We rent the scanners anywhere from an hour up to a week to people who want to scan photos fast. Clients who rent typically can scan around 500 photos per hour. Rentals come with the scanner, a laptop, and optional flatbed accessory.

Nationwide, people can rent the scanners through E-Z Photo with its Rent2Scan program. This company is the go-to expert in renting and supporting scanners to consumers around the country.

You can find their contact information in the Resources at the end of this book.

Our local FOX television station featured us on air demonstrating the PS80. Many people have no idea this scanning equipment exists. It was fun to tell the world there is an easier way to scan photos!

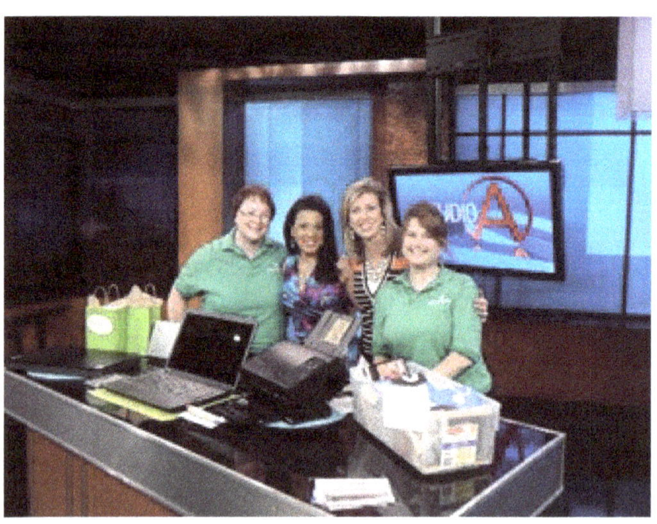

After reviewing the types of scanners that are available, does the thought of scanning photos overwhelm you? That's okay.

HIRE SOMEONE TO SCAN YOUR PHOTOS

There are many providers who will scan your photos for you. Most options involve shipping your photos somewhere to have the work done. This can be nerve-wracking for some people who worry the photos may be lost in the journey.

We have several locations around the country. Check to see if there is a Pixologie near you.

Another great resource is the Association of Personal Photo Organizers. If you are looking for someone locally to help you scan photos, go to www.appo.org. You will find resources and a directory of personal photo organizers around the country.

When you hire someone to help you with your photo projects, we recommend asking for two references. If you are using an online scanning service, please Google its name and read their reviews.

Best Practices for Your Photos *(Appendix B)* offers recommendations for saving your photos and other media.

Saving Your Scanned Photos

Now that we've covered scanning options, let's discuss how to save the scanned photos to your computer. When scanning, create folders for your photos based on the categories by which you sorted them.

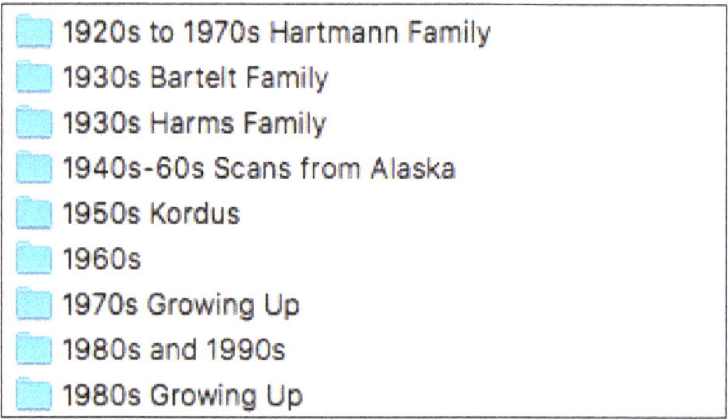

Screen shot of scanned picture folders.

Creating Two Back-Ups of Your Photos

Once you have scanned your photos, you'll have your original digital files stored on your computer. We recommend that two copies be made. One copy can be stored in your home, and the other should be stored outside of your home. Having copies in two locations ensures your photos are safe, even if you have a disaster at home.

FIRST COPY: Simply copy your scanned photos to an external hard drive. Remember to update your back-up on the external hard drive if you scan additional photos on your computer.

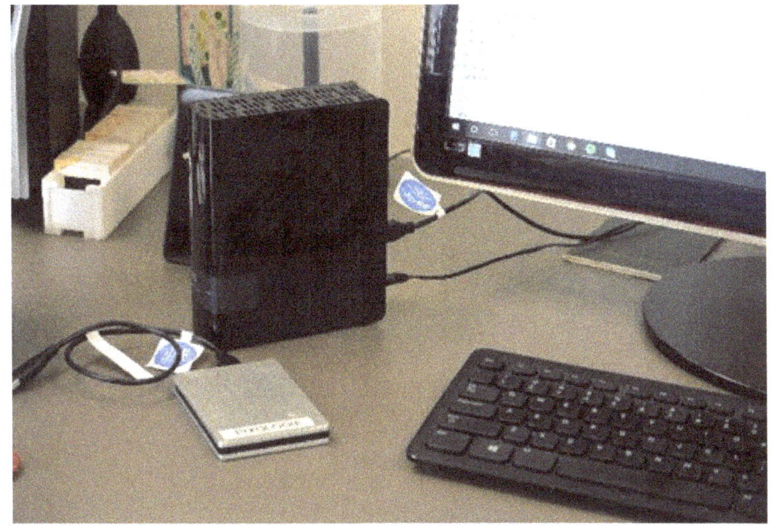

Here are two types of external hard drives, one small portable and one large desktop drive. Either one will work for your in-home back-up.

SECOND COPY: This copy should be stored outside of your home. Several options for the safekeeping of your second copy include:

- A second external hard drive. Store it in a safe deposit box or at a relative's home.
- Cloud back-up. There are many computer back-up services available including Carbonite and Backblaze. These services back up all your computer's files.

  In the event of a computer crash, the company will send your files back for you to restore to your computer.

Cautionary note: *Please do not depend upon a cloud service being your ONLY photo back-up. While Carbonite and Backblaze have been around a long time, many technology companies have come and gone. Also, we have heard client stories where the back-up they counted on did not work properly and photos were lost.*

- Photo-specific cloud services: Google Photos and Amazon Photos are two free services available, among many others. I'll be addressing these free services later in the book. We prefer to use a private photo storage account called Forever. Here's a little bit about Forever from its website:

  With Forever, you can edit, organize, store, and share your photos. Rest easy knowing your content will always be safe in your permanent digital home at Forever. All of this is possible because of the Forever Guarantee and our easy-to-use web, mobile, and desktop apps.

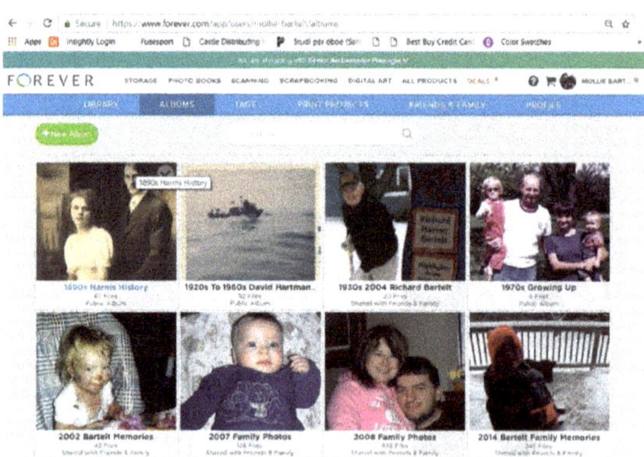

Screen shot of my Forever account. It's fun to see the digital albums of my scanned photos.

We have covered a lot of topics related to managing the chaos of our printed photos including:

- Why we should save our printed photos
- What tools we need to organize our photos
- What photos we should keep
- How to organize our photos
- How to save our photos by creating digital back-ups

The vast majority of our clients report they have a digital mess of photos, as well as their printed pictures. Now that we have created digital photos of our printed pictures, let's talk about how to save digital photos in the next chapter.

"Take care of your memories, for you cannot relive them."

—Bob Dylan

CHAPTER SIX

HOW TO SAVE YOUR DIGITAL PHOTOS

Although this book is primarily about printed photo organization, I did want to address digital photo management for a few moments. Remember how we brought all our printed pictures to one location? We want to do the same thing for our digital photos. This means bringing our scanned photos together with our digital photos.

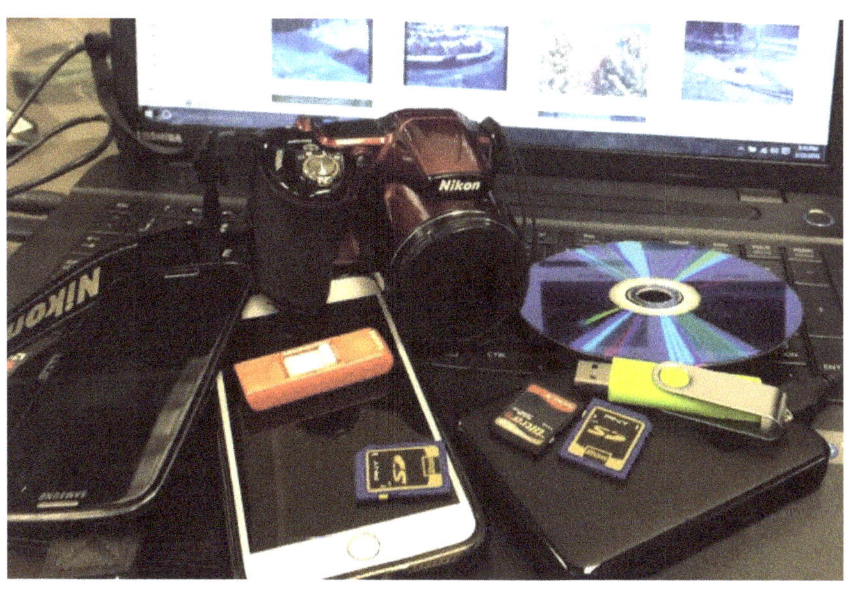

Here's a brief list of where you'll be grabbing all the digital photos you want to keep:

- Laptop computer
- Desktop computer
- Smartphone (camera, text messages)
- External hard drive
- Jump drives/thumb drives
- DVDs/CDs
- Email
- Social media (Facebook, Instagram)
- Camera/Camera SD Cards

Bringing All the Digital Photos Together

While cloud-based solutions are numerous, some consumers are not yet ready to embrace the cloud. The most common place we see people storing their digital photos is on computers, smartphones, and in social media accounts. We need to bring all the digital photos together in one place if we want to get rid of our digital mess!

Today, the most logical place to save your digital photo collection is on your personal computer. You need to make a strong effort to transfer photos from your smartphone, social media accounts, and camera to your computer on a routine basis.

We recommend, at a minimum, that you bring your photos to your computer at the end of each month. For both

PC and Mac computers, you should store your photos in the "Pictures" folder.

You can do much more with your photos than simply getting them to one place where they can be backed up. PCs and Macs offer free photo software solutions that allow you to correct red eyes, crop your pictures, and add metadata to your photos.

- PC—Photo Gallery, Photos (Will vary depending upon which version of Windows your computer is using.)
- Mac—Photos (also includes facial recognition)

There are many online videos to watch so you can learn how to get the most out of these programs. You can also find community classes to take as well.

For people who want even more power to work with their photos (facial recognition, advanced editing, and adding metadata), we've used these programs with our clients as well:

- Forever Historian (PC)
- Mylio (PC and Mac)
- Creative Cloud—Photoshop, Lightroom, Bridge (PC and Mac. For advanced users)
- Forever Guaranteed Storage (PC and Mac)

Steps for Saving Your Digital Photos

At least monthly, follow these steps to save your digital photos:

- Bring all your photos together to a folder on your computer.
- Name your folder by the month you are working on: YYYY-MM (example: 2018-10 Photos)
- Delete the ones you don't want. RIGHT AWAY!
- Back up your photos twice (one copy saved in the house; one copy saved outside the house)

Think of all the times you may have taken a photo and just shared your photo through social media or a text. Many, many photos have been lost because people take their photos, maybe share the photos, and never get them organized or properly backed up.

Follow the system so you can put your hands on a picture when you need it, digitally speaking!

Naming Your Digital File Folders

I want to expand on how to name your digital file folders. This is important if you are tackling your digital photo mess, beyond just saving your photos on a monthly basis.

We recommend the naming convention of YYYY-MM-DD - Description, which will help your folders display in date order. The year always comes first. For example:

- 2014-12-10 Christmas Concert
- 2014-12 December Phone Photos

Name	Date Modified
2015-05 Hannah's Band Concert	Mar 12, 2016, 7:28 PM
2015-05 Junior National Honor Society	Aug 8, 2015, 4:53 PM
2015-05 Other May Photos	Mar 12, 2016, 7:28 PM
2015-05 Tammy's House	Jun 1, 2015, 2:14 PM
2015-06 Alex Rides a Bike	Jan 31, 2016, 6:09 PM
2015-06 June Photos	Aug 3, 2015, 9:12 PM
2015-07 Hannah's Band Camp	Oct 24, 2015, 8:37 PM
2015-07 July Photos	Nov 27, 2015, 5:18 PM
2015-07 Trip to Alaska	Nov 27, 2015, 5:01 PM
2015-07-01 Alex Testing	Aug 3, 2015, 7:46 PM
2015-07-11 Family Reunion	Oct 24, 2015, 9:37 PM
2015-08 August Photos	May 28, 2016, 9:48 PM
2015-08 Last Day of Summer Vacation	Oct 24, 2015, 8:10 PM
2015-08 Magnolia Ridge	Nov 27, 2015, 5:59 PM
2015-08 Salon Day	Dec 28, 2015, 7:50 PM

Listing of file folders from a MacBook Pro.
File folders were named by date and photos were split up into events.

Adding Scanned Photos to Your Digital Collection

You may be wondering how to add your scanned photos to your digital collection. Depending on your computer savvy and your desire, you can:

- Leave the scanned pictures separate from your other digital folders in your Pictures File
- Create dated folders and move your scanned photos into the years they belong
- Import the scanned photos into your photo management software

The possibilities are endless due to the huge number of photo editing software and apps available for consumers. Here's a screenshot from a PC of folders with scanned pictures in them. By putting the year first, they are automatically organized chronologically.

1925 Hartmann History, Dad Photos	8/14/2016 7:24 AM	File folder
1930s, Misc. Bartelt Historical Photos	8/14/2016 7:24 AM	File folder
1940s-60s Scans from Alaska	8/14/2016 7:24 AM	File folder
1950s Kordus	8/14/2016 7:24 AM	File folder
1960s	8/14/2016 7:24 AM	File folder
1970s Growing Up	8/14/2016 7:24 AM	File folder

Screen shot of folders organized by year to combine scanned and digital photos.

Backing Up Your Digital Photos

As with backing up your scanned photos, we recommend two backups of your computer's digital photo collection.

FIRST COPY – Copy your Pictures file to an external hard drive. Remember to update your backup on the external hard drive every time you add photos to your Pictures file.

SECOND COPY – Should be stored outside of your home.

A couple of options include a second external hard drive and/or Cloud backup as discussed in Chapter Five.

iCloud

With many, many consumers using iPhones and iPads to take pictures, I would like to point out a few things about iCloud.

- Every iPhone and iPad owner has an iCloud account.
- You can go to icloud.com and use your Apple ID to log into your account. By clicking on the Photos icon, you will see your photos stored in iCloud.

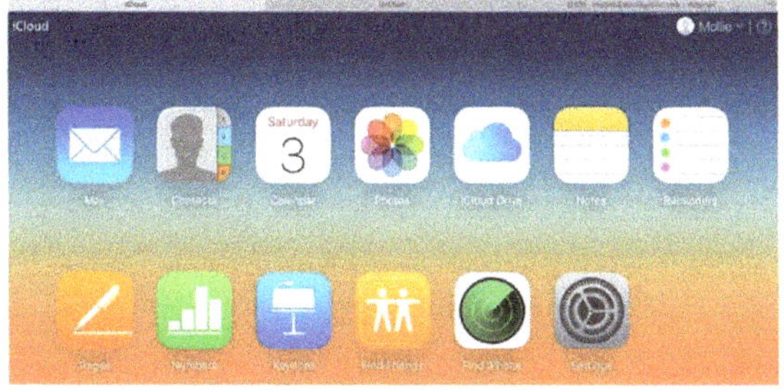

iCloud control panel.

- I have seen people with multiple iCloud accounts because they have signed up through different devices with different email accounts. Be sure you are using the same iCloud account for all your devices.
- For iCloud to backup your photos on your iPhone and iPad, you must turn on the backup feature in Photos. If you don't have enough storage, you will be prompted to upgrade. The iCloud Photo Library cannot be turned on because there is not enough storage available.
- iCloud offers 5 GB of free storage. If you wish to purchase more storage, Apple offers a reasonable price of 99 cents per month for 50 GB more of storage.

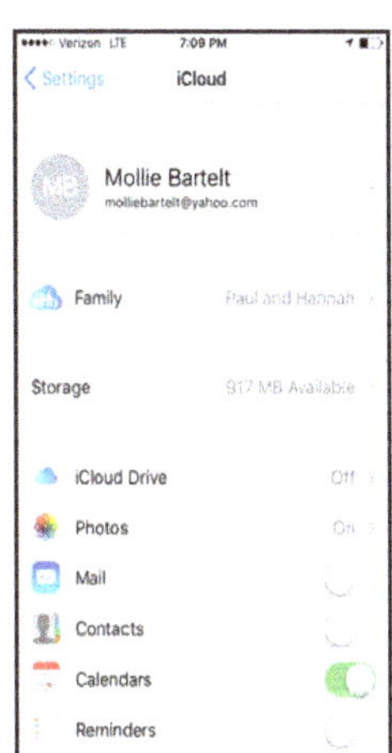

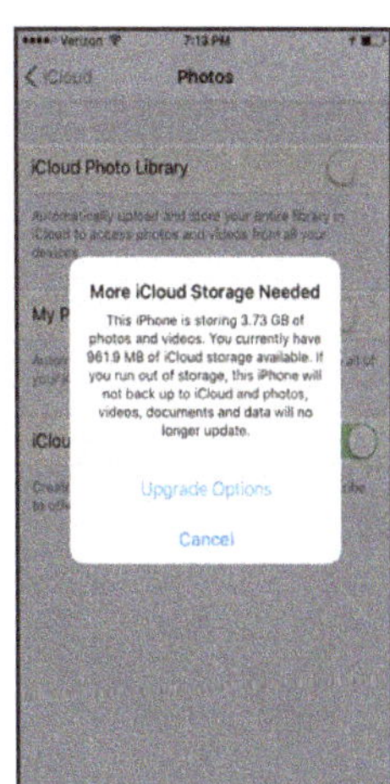

- The photos that are in your iCloud library are an exact copy of what is on your phone, iPad, and computer (if you use Mac Photos). When you delete a photo, you are deleting it from all of your devices.

Other Online or "Cloud" Storage

For people who use PCs, the internet offers "free" cloud storage for photos, including Google. We caution our clients about these websites for reasons including:

- A wise saying states that if something is free, you are not the consumer, you are the product. Some "free" sites pay for storing your photos by selling your information or even access to your photos. If you use one of these sites, be sure to review the agreement and make sure you are not signing away the rights to your personal photos.
- With the fast mergers, changes and closures that occur in technology companies, the website may not be around in a few years. We have had clients lose access to their photos because the company closed or merged with another company and service ended for online photo storage.

"Forever" Storage

I routinely recommend that people consider *Forever*, the permanent photo storage company mentioned previously. You can purchase 10GB of storage for a one-time fee of $199 which can hold 2,500 to 5,000 photos. A portion of that purchase goes into the "Forever" Guarantee Fund, which promises to migrate your photos to the newest technology for the next 100 years.

Keep in mind that you still need to have a full copy in your home. Find more information in the Resource section at the end of the book.

Below is one album from my Forever account, in which I have stored the heritage photos of my dad.

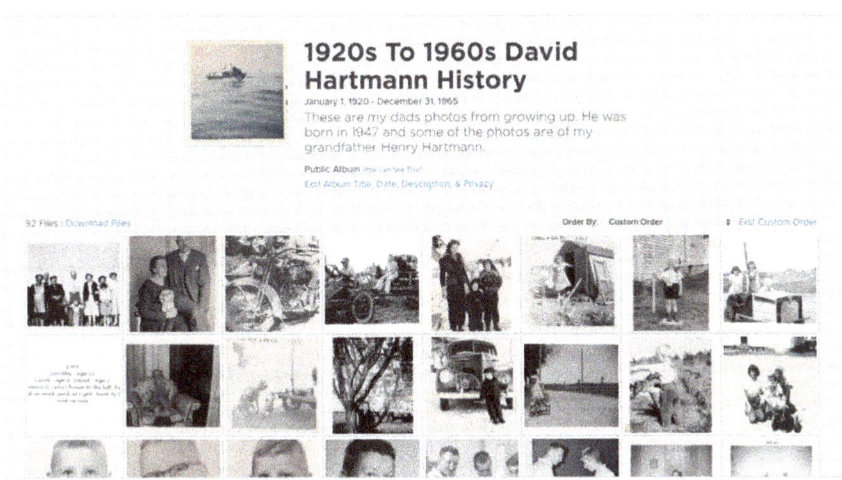

I wrote this book as a simple guide to saving photos. To keep this book short and sweet, I limited the scope of this chapter to the basics of digital photo organization, a topic worthy of its own guide.

Note: You can learn more about Forever by visiting www.forever.com/ambassador/pixologie to start a free trial account.

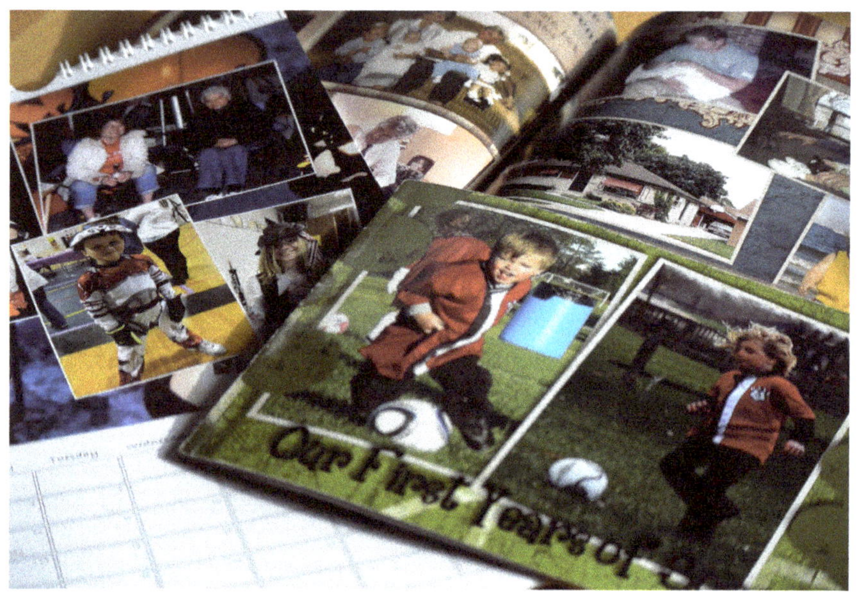

After the mess.

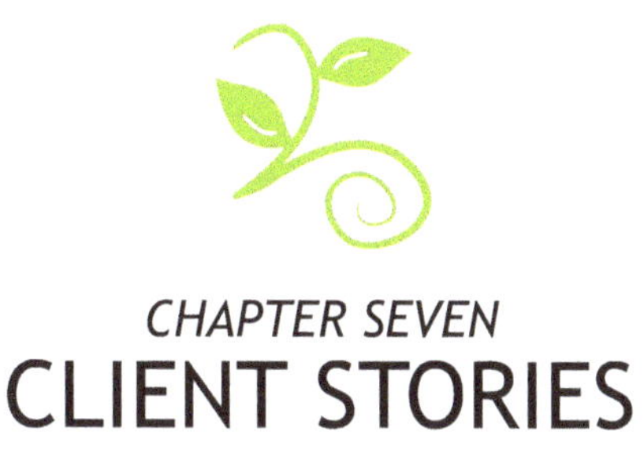

CHAPTER SEVEN

CLIENT STORIES

Throughout the book, I have described how we help clients sort their photos. Would you like to see what kind of projects we have seen?

SAVING A FAMILY LEGACY

Kelly had a photo dilemma in her home. With her young family, her own photos needed help. But before she could consider working on those, she had to deal with two other large collections of old, printed photos. Remember the photo below from earlier in the book? Kelly had her grandmother's photo collection and her mother's photo collection. She hired us to get both collections sorted and preserved. Let's walk through the sorting and saving process.

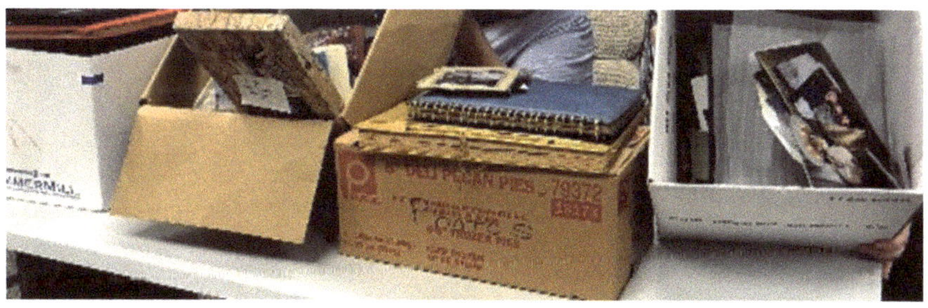

In addition to the albums, envelopes and frames, some of the boxes held loose photos.

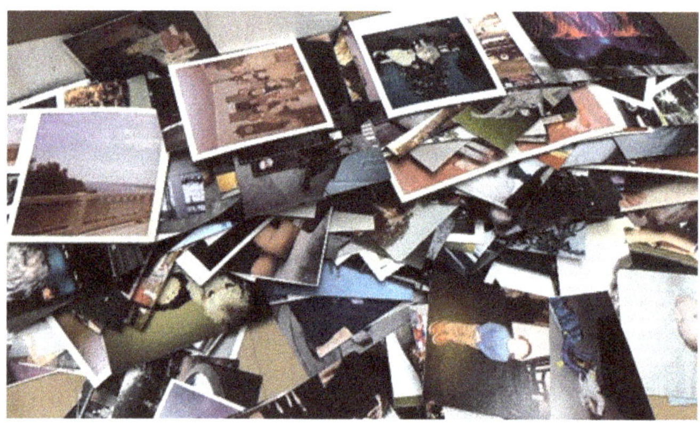

So we did the first sorting by major category.

- Left front box – Grandmother's photos sorted by decade
- Left back box – Grandmother's professionally framed photos, memorabilia
- Right front box – Mother's photos sorted by decade (with a few years as well due to albums being labeled). portraits in the back.
- Right back box – Empty photo albums
- Notice the blue cases – Reels of 8mm film were mixed in with the photos.

(See photo next page.)

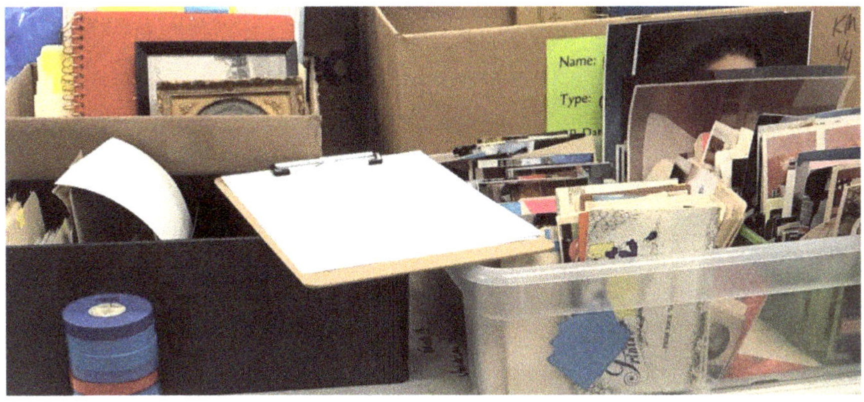

Next, we broke down her mother's photos by years. Each sticky note has a year from the 1970s on it and we are simply stacking photos on the corresponding year (Found by markings on the back of the photos, etc.) The stacks in the bin are sorted by 1940s, 1950s, 1960, 1961 through 1969.

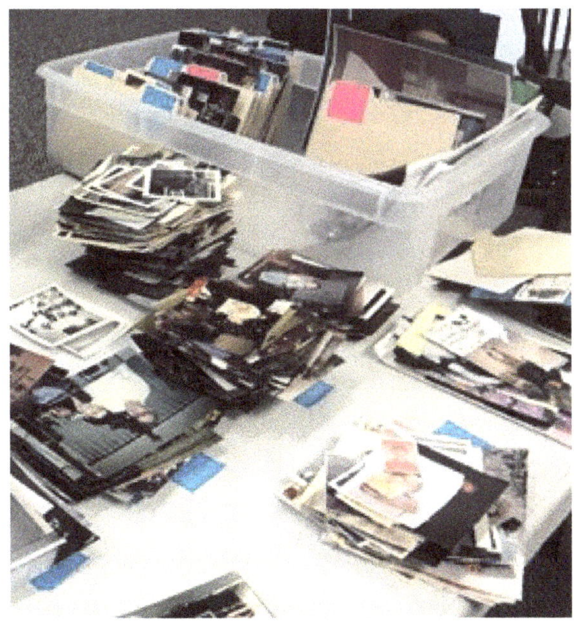

Duplicates, repetitive photos were removed as they were found.

Final, organized photos were placed in archival boxes with printed labels. The envelope standing up contains the oversized photos. The reference cards refer to when an oversized photo can be found in the envelope. Both Kelly's grandmother's and mother's photo collections are contained in the Legacy Box— about 2,300 photos.

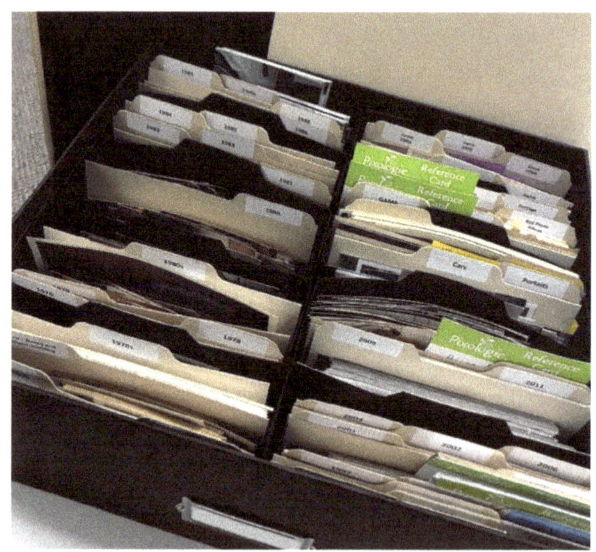

We then scanned her photos and uploaded them to a Forever account and provided her with copies on jump drives to save to her computer.

"You Have Restored My Life"

Remember the retired attorney who contacted us needing a "Pixologist"? Gen had many boxes, albums, bags, envelopes, and more of photos, slides, and even 8mm film. Here are the Before photos:

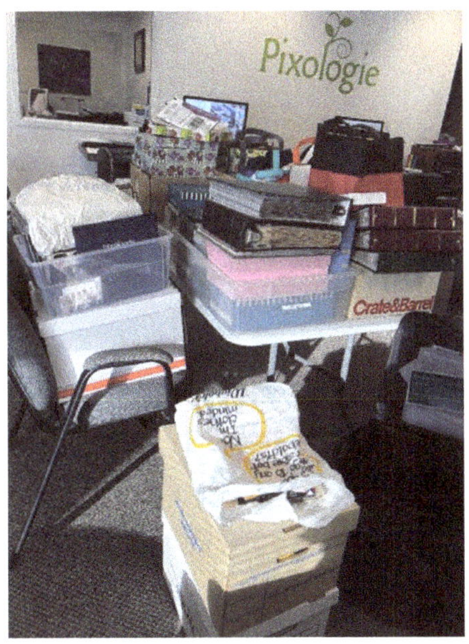

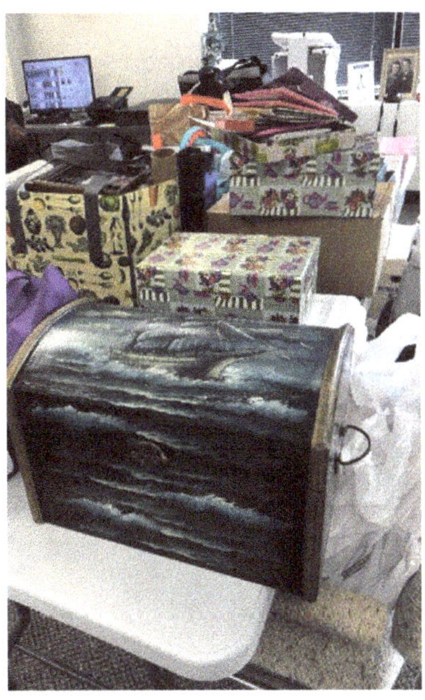

***After the first sorting by decade*:** You can see that we have separated the slides out and left photos in the envelopes to start with. Once we could see all the envelopes, it was easy to sort the envelopes by date and then remove the photos from the envelopes.

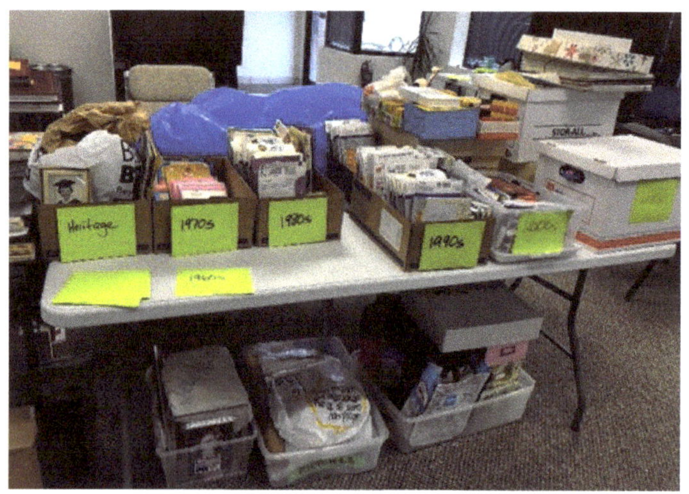

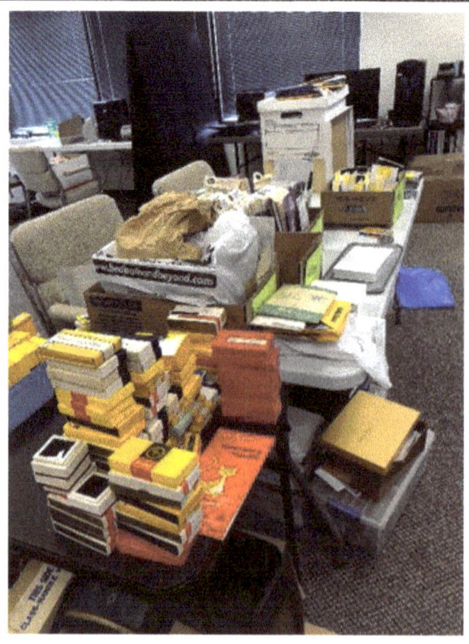

Below, we are sorting the heritage photos. See the oversized negatives on the bottom right? Those were set aside to be reviewed later. We found many duplicates.

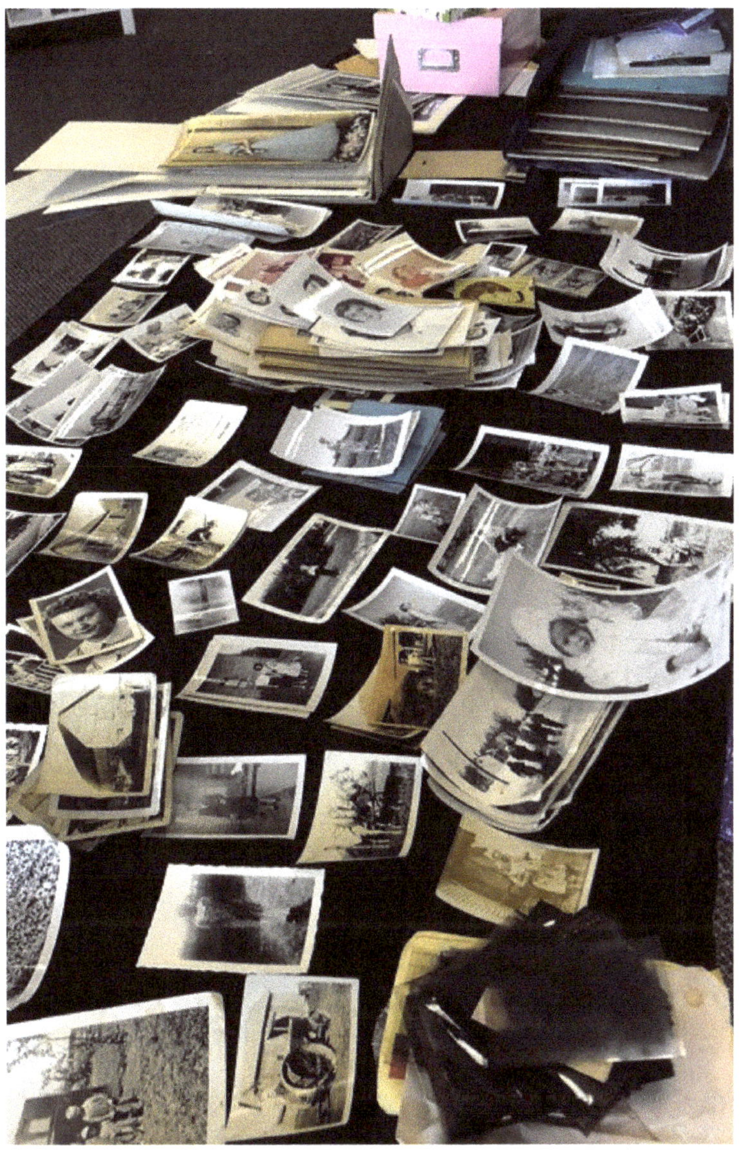

Because we had gone through Gen's boxes and consolidated her heritage photos, we were able to match up photos taken on the same day. We kept the ones in better condition and eliminated the duplicates.

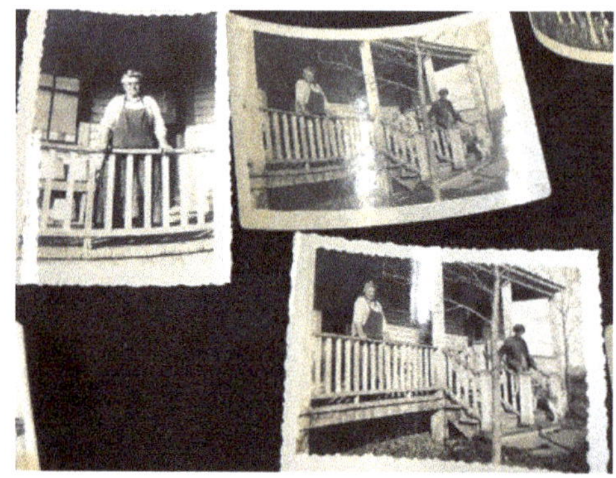

Here's the next phase of her project . . . decades sorted by years, slides and film digitized as well. Now, the photos are awaiting archival boxes for storage, if Gen choses to save her printed collection.

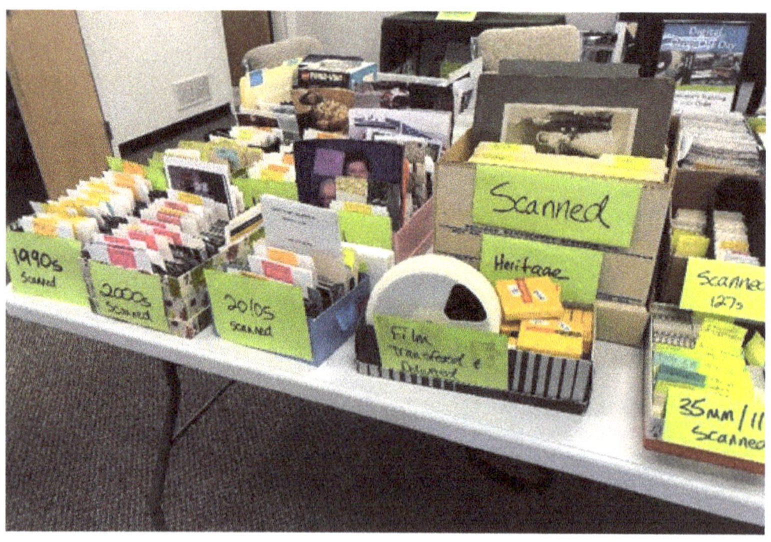

Organized and Digitized:

- Scanned Photos – 5,972
- Slides – 1,700 or so
- Film – 29 reels
- VHS tape – 1

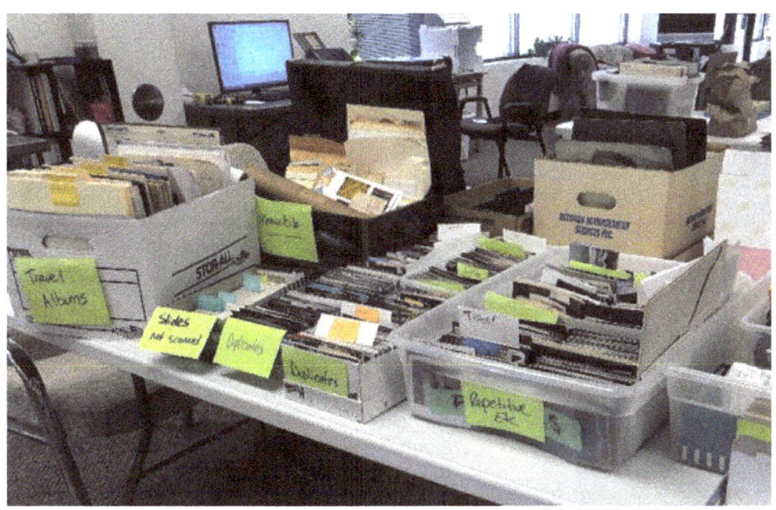

Not Digitized:

- Duplicates & repetitive, unnecessary photos – around 8,000
- Travel memorabilia – I did scan a few items from some of the major trips
- Slides – around 500
- Memorabilia – large trunk filled

Gen has been so appreciative of being able to enjoy her photos again. I uploaded her photos to a Forever Account and she is able to view her pictures on her iPad, reliving many long-forgotten memories. She feels so blessed at looking back over the photos, stating "I've had a fairytale life. You have restored it!"

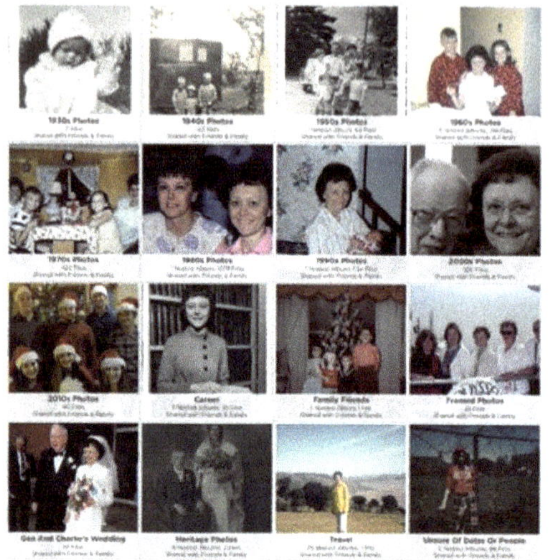

Photos below of her Travel Album. She also preserved her heritage photos from two generations before her.

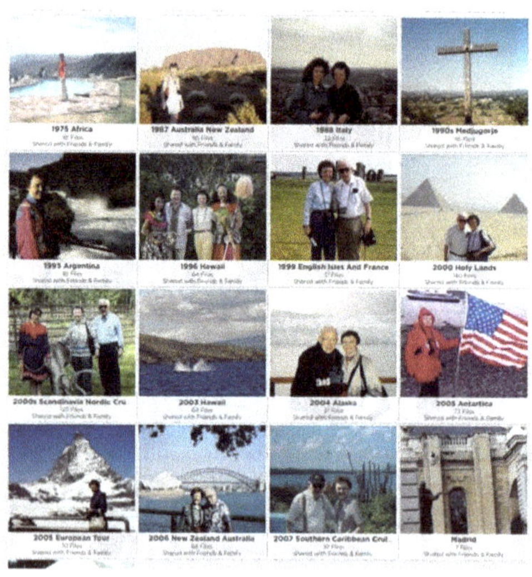

Her next plans are to have photobooks printed so that she can enjoy easily looking through her memories in print!

A Full Photo Closet

Lori has her own successful business helping her clients create beautiful scrapbooks and digital photo books—a calling she loves. But, something in Lori's house was also calling her: a photo closet full of more than 20,000 (our eyeball guesstimate) printed photos that needed to be scanned before she could create scrapbooks of her own family's heritage.

Psychologically, her chaos of photos might as well have been mountains, it was so overwhelming.

She wrote to us, "Not only do I have decades of old photos, and take hundreds/thousands of photos each year, but I also acquired heritage photos from my dad, Pat's parents, and Pat's grandmother dating into the 1800s."

Here's what she listed in her collection:

- Her father's photo albums (back row on table): 15+
- Photo boxes with 2400 photos in each of them: 6
- Banker's boxes stuffed full of developed photos and memorabilia: 8
- CDs of photos
- Files and additional boxes filled with photos: 4+
- And many more

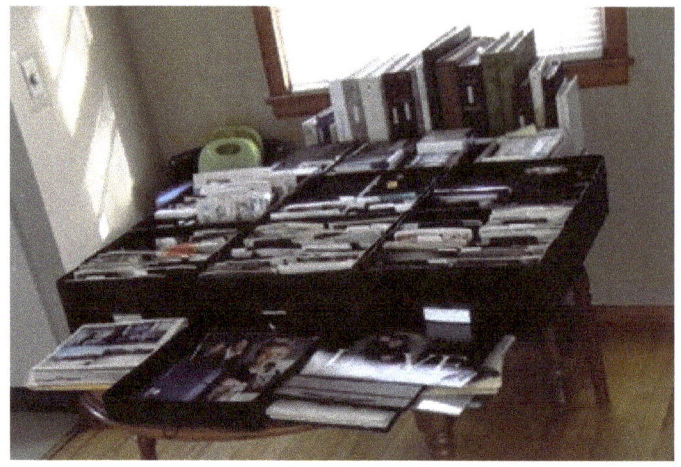

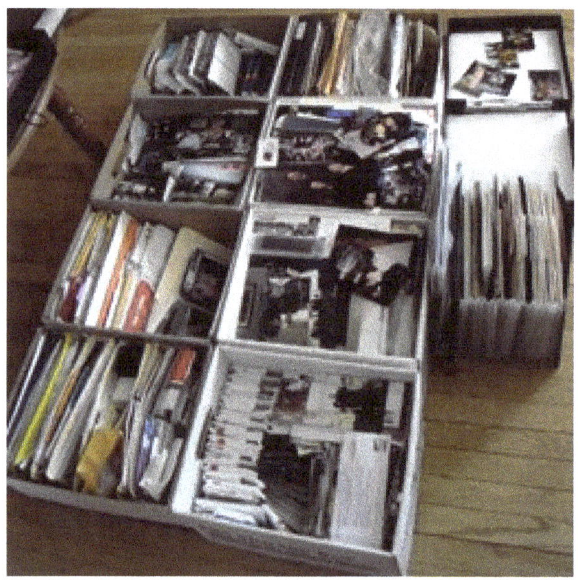

As you can see from the photos, Lori's pictures were well organized and ready for scanning.

Frustrated, Lori stopped scrapbooking because she wanted to back up the only copy of these photos digitally before she put them into albums. With that process being tedious and time-consuming on her flatbed scanner, she was getting farther and farther behind.

Lori made the decision to rent the scanner to use for an extended period. With the scanner rental, Lori worked at her pace in the comfort of her own home.

She said, "Approaching this project methodically has been helpful. It is not only fine tuning the photo-sorting process, it's also helping me get more organized and record family information."

Below you can see how methodical she was with her work station set up in her office.

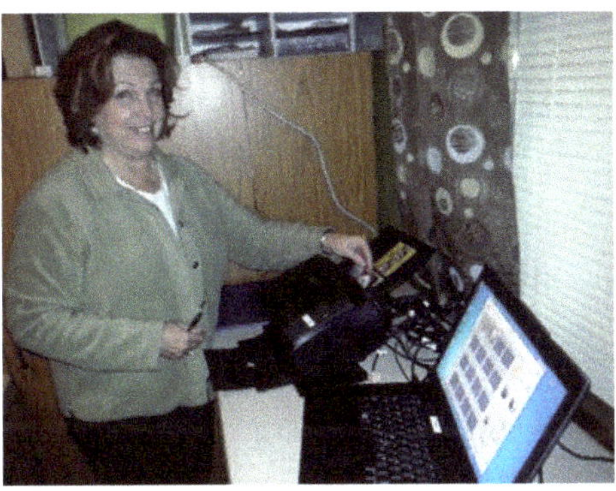

Lori was very happy to have a fast solution for her photo closet, and she scanned thousands of photos over the course of several weeks.

Eileen's Favorite Memory of Being 83

My mother-in-law Eileen and her niece Susan spent a few hours each week over the course of fourteen months working on a large photo project. First, they sorted through old photos from Susan's side of the family, identifying grandparents and great-grandparents along with other relatives.

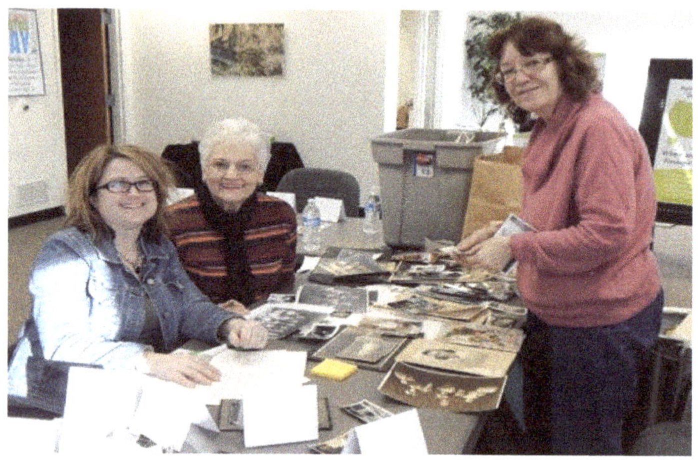

Then I helped them scan the photos so they could work on creating a digital photo book of the Kruger/Krueger/Bartelt family history. It was great when Eileen and Susan were sorting photos because they laughed so often and clearly enjoyed spending the time together reminiscing.

When Eileen celebrated her 84th birthday year a few months later, she was asked, "What was your favorite memory from being 83?" After thinking a bit, Eileen replied, "All the time working with Susan, Mollie, and those photos!"

In the photo below, they are working on the last page of their digital photo book. And someday, Susan's granddaughter Grace will treasure looking at the book with her family's history and photos. That is how photos connect the generations.

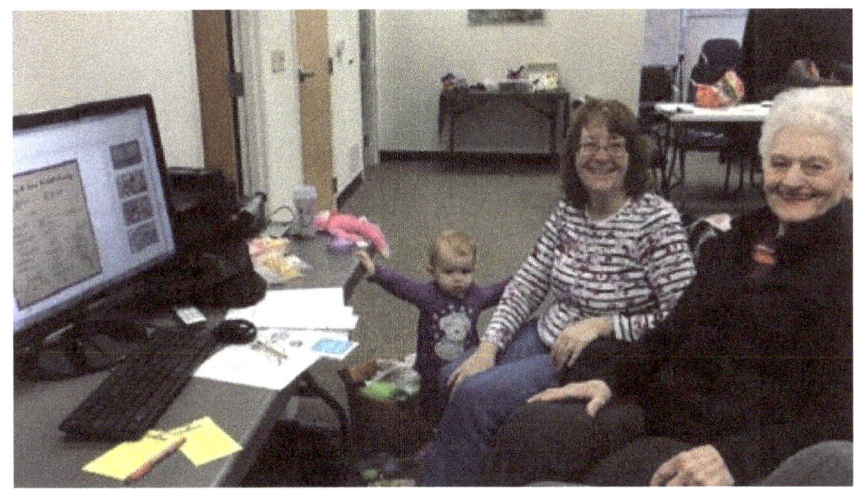

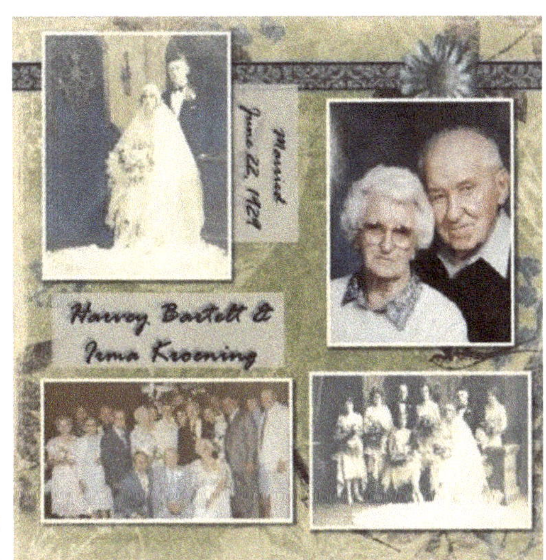

A page out of the photo book Eileen and Susan created.

"People are taking more pictures than ever before, billions of them. But there's no slides, no prints, just data, electronic dust. Years from now, when they dig us up, there won't be any pictures to find. No record of who we were, how we lived."

—Ben Ryder

(Played by actor Ed Harris in the movie *Kodachrome)*

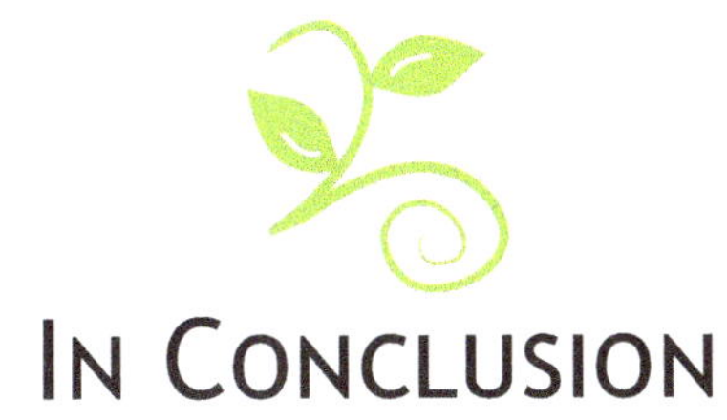

In Conclusion

Well, we have covered so much in this book. I truly hope you have found our system to be helpful and that you can make it work for you. I have had people take my classes and get right to work, and others still need time to process what they need to do.

My book publisher, Kira Henschel, is also pondering what to do with her printed photo collection and how (when) she will start to save the memories. She had a great suggestion: "Find a photo buddy." This is a great idea. It is so much more fun to work with someone who wants to also save photos. Kira hopes her sister and daughter will join her.

Having a photo buddy can work a couple of ways. Perhaps work with a family member to organize and save the best photos. Be sure to not get caught up in reminiscing, or it will take longer!

We have also had photo workshops and crops at the Pixologie office, where people bring their photo projects to us. The social environment is fun, yet people still work on their own projects. Having a dedicated time and place outside of the house might be the difference in completing your organization project or not. We have found that some of our clients enjoy getting away for the weekend to work on projects.

However you approach your photo organization project, please know that I am rooting for you, cheering for you, and hoping for heaps of blessings to you! Enjoy your memories once again!

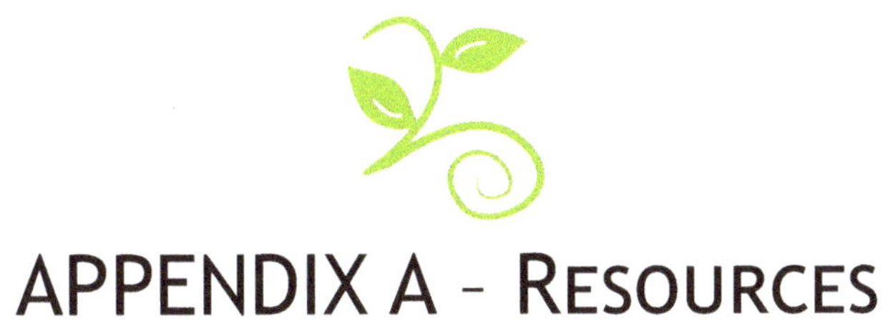

APPENDIX A - RESOURCES

Photo Organizing Tips, Videos, Articles & More

Pixologie

www.pixologieinc.com
Telephone: 414-731-1881
Email: mollieb@pixologieinc.com
Click on the Pixologist tools for free downloads, worksheets and more. Purchase Flip Pal Scanners, Legacy Boxes and other tools for your project. Also find our other locations.

The Association of Personal Photo Organizers

www.appo.com
In addition to a variety of resources and motivation, find a photo organizer near you

E-Z Photo

Powered by i/o Track, Inc.
www.ezphoto.cc
Telephone: 866-468-7250

Forever

www.forever.com
Products including permanent photo storage, photobook software and much more. Please select Pixologie, Oak Creek, WI as we'd love to be your ambassador and be connected to you. We do receive a commission on sales.

Genealogy Resources

Family Tree Magazine
https://www.familytreemagazine.com/premium/websites-for-old-family-photos/
Read through the article for different sites where you can upload photos that you cannot identify.

Maureen Taylor, the Photo Detective
https://maureentaylor.com/
Great resource for learning more about very old photos.

APPENDIX B: BEST PRACTICES FOR YOUR MEMORIES

There are too many options for consumers, too many ways to save a photo and too little time to figure it out. Over the past two years, at Pixologie, we have done a deep dive into developing photo organization standards, digital file format best practices, and levels of service.

I have broken down our best practices into **Preservation** and **Archival** levels. Following these descriptions, I discuss the Consumer Level of service.

PRESERVATION LEVEL

- Generally for consumers, family photo collections
- Printed photos are sorted, stored in photo-safe, archival-quality boxes
- Scanned photos are 300 or 600 dpi, saved as superior, quality JPGs
- Digital photos are saved as JPGs
- Slides and negatives are scanned at 2000 dpi and saved as JPGs
- Videos and film are transferred to a digital file – MP4
- Back-up includes two digital copies, one onsite (off the main computer) and one offsite

Archival Level

- For professional photographers, business and historical photo collections
- Printed photos, slides, negatives are sorted, stored in photo-safe, archival-quality boxes
- Scanned photos are 600 dpi, saved as TIFFs, once edits completed, can be saved as JPGs
- Digital files are tagged, dates are corrected
- Slides and negatives are scanned at 4000 DPI
- Videos and film are remastered, saved as AVI or MOV
- Back-up includes two digital copies, one onsite (off the main computer) and one offsite

We at Pixologie are committed to educating consumers and our clients on what standards will best preserve their memories for the future. However, these levels of service do come at a higher price point. When we find that clients are looking for a lower cost solution, there is an additional level of service: the Consumer Level.

Consumer Level

Many times, people access consumer levels of service because they are unaware there are other options and considerations to ensure their photos and family movies will be around for generations to come. Some consumers do choose to have a lower cost service and are willing to compromise on the quality of service.

- Photos are scanned on flatbed scanners with unknown DPI and quality
- Digital files are saved on DVDs and jump drives with no consideration of how the photo will be organized and found later
- Slides and negatives are scanned using a consumer-grade scanner with inconsistent color correction and unknown resolution
- Videos and film are transferred to lower size and quality digital formats (MP4s or MPGs) or transferred and compressed straight to a DVD

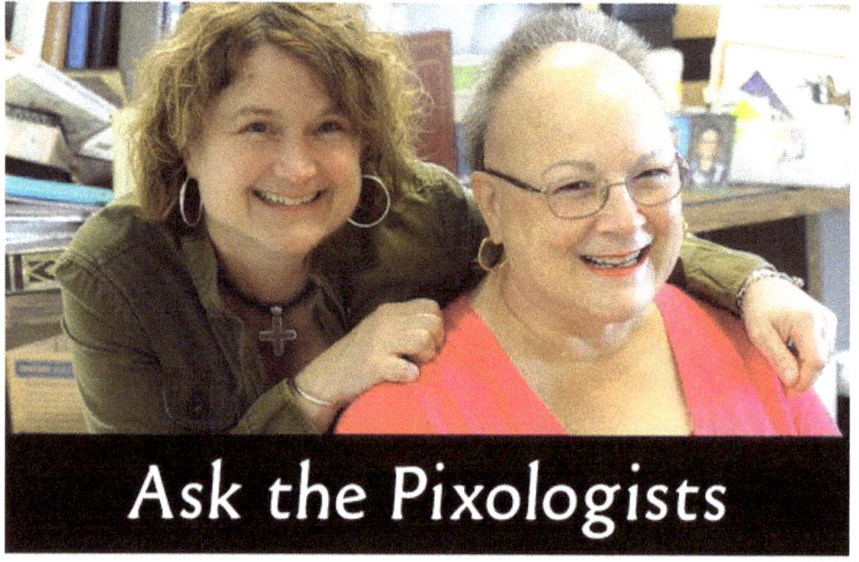

Pixologists Mollie Bartelt and Ann Matuszak

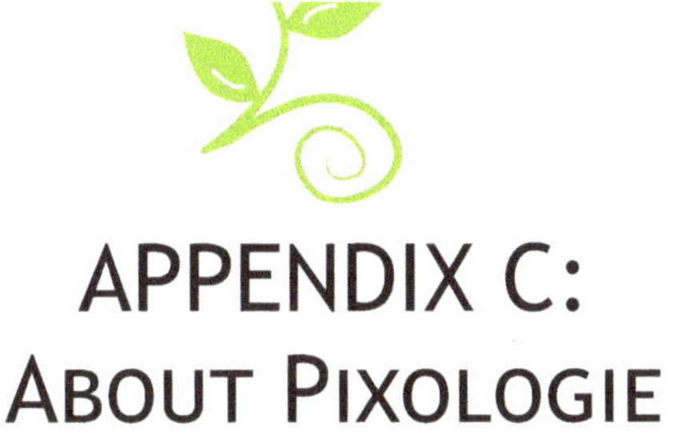

APPENDIX C: ABOUT PIXOLOGIE

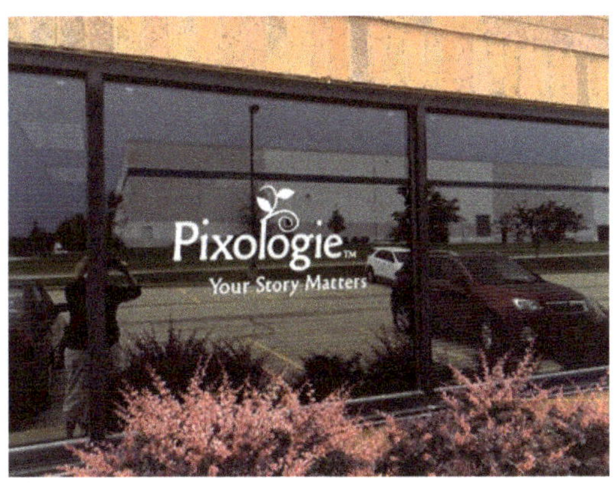

A photo and media organization and management business, Pixologie was founded in 2013 by Mollie Bartelt and Ann Matuszak because they love photos and the stories that are captured in them. They believe that relationships and lives can be improved when individuals and families celebrate their memories and traditions by looking through their photos together.

Bringing a wealth of non-profit business management, direct sales, and social service experience, Ann and Mollie believe photo and media organization services offers individuals, families, and even organizations and businesses, a place to start and the tools to preserve their photos.

Pixologie, Inc. is located in the greater Milwaukee, Wisconsin area and is unique in offering photo organization and management services along with onsite do-it-yourself options for our clients.

Phone: (414) 731-1881
Address: 9803 S. 13th Street
Oak Creek, WI 53154
Website: www.pixologieinc.com

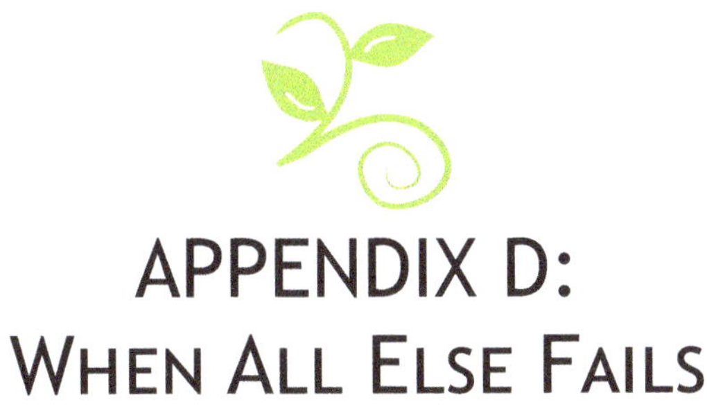

APPENDIX D: When All Else Fails

Okay, you've been through this book a few times and you're still stuck. Is it time to considering hiring a photo organizer or pixologist? Here are a few scenarios to consider and if any apply to you, you might need to hire a photo organizer.

Printed photos are scattered throughout the home in old albums, boxes, baggies and envelopes.

- Digital photos are in more than three places (smartphone, email, computer, etc.)
- Organizing your photos has been on your to-do list for more than one year.
- Your backup plan is sketchy. HINT: If you don't have your original digital photos backed up in two places including one location outside of your house...this applies to you :)

I frequently hear that people are waiting for the right time to work on their photos. But time flies by, even years, and the photos accumulate. Then a life event happens and you need the photos in a hurry for a graduation, wedding, or funeral.

These are stressful times to be searching through boxes of photos and scanning your computer files to find pictures.

Why Hire a Photo Organizer?

Here are some advantages of having a photo organizer help you with your printed or digital photo mess.

Photo organizers:

- Are efficient and work without the distractions that take people away from their photo projects (family calls, housework, etc.)
- Have a system to sort photos by major categories (determined with you), setting aside duplicates, negatives, memorabilia and other items for your review
- Don't reminisce about the photos as they work and are objective partners in your project
- Can complete your photo organization project in just a matter of days or weeks in most cases

Here's why Diane hired Pixologie to organize her photos, which are shown on the next page. *"Every time I was asked for a picture, whether for school or something else, I shuddered. I was overwhelmed. I couldn't believe how Mollie condensed and organized and labeled them. She got my mess down to a very manageable amount of boxes."*

The "after" photo shows what Diane's photos looked like after I organized them for her. It took me just 11 hours to objectively fly through using the age chart for her children.

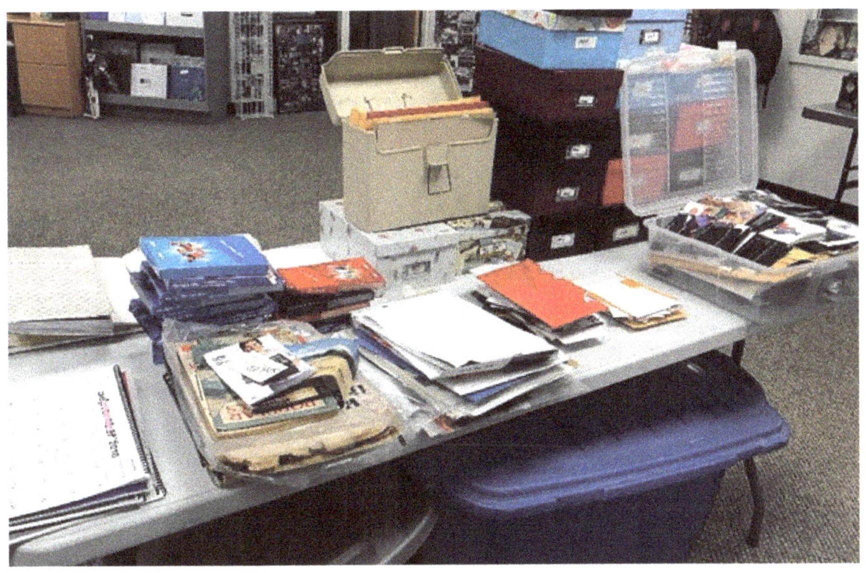

Before (above) and after (below)

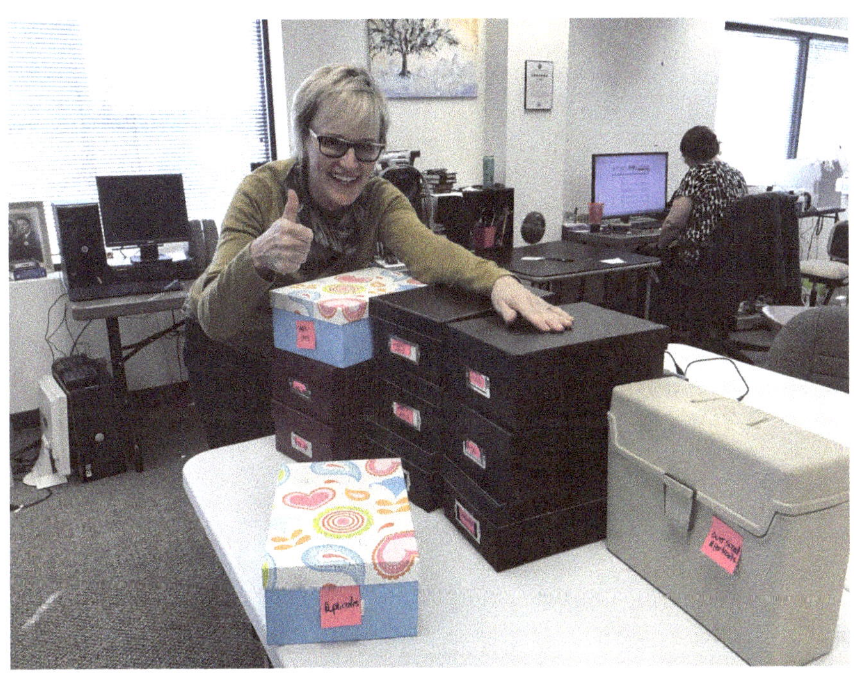

She now has nine boxes of photos, as well as a file box with the oversized photos. The box in the front contains the duplicates.

If you are ready to hire a photo organizer, refer back to the Resources Appendix. Please don't hesitate to drop me a line if I can be a resource! Go enjoy your memories again. Your photos are calling you and they have so much to say!

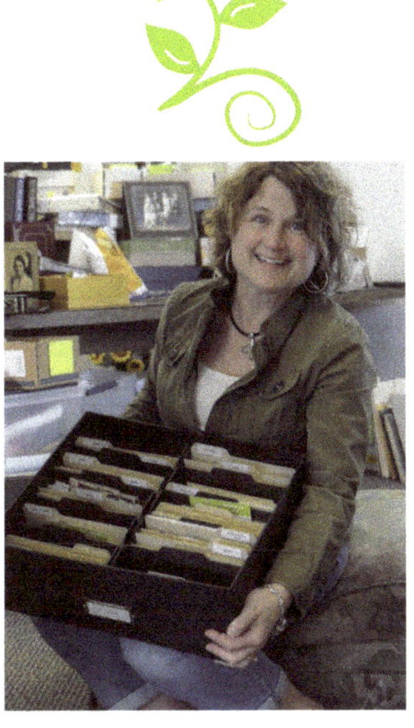

About the Author

Mollie Bartelt—photo organizer, Pixologist, mission-driven entrepreneur—is on a mission to save people's stories and ensure future generations have a meaningful photographic family history.

Mollie's career started in the nonprofit, healthcare and assisted living fields, where she ran adult day centers and other community programs to help older adults remain living in the community. Even back then, she saw the value of family photographs and photo albums as a comfort and memory tool for her clients.

Along the way, Mollie joined a direct sales business in the memory-saving field and sold scrapbooks, photo albums, and digital photobook software. She loved creating books for her children to look through and see all the family had done together.

In fact, one summer, while her husband was unemployed, Mollie remembers Labor Day coming and school starting. She felt terrible because, with limited finances, the family hadn't been able to do much. However, over that weekend, she caught up the family album with summer pictures and realized how much the family had done . . . from campfires in the backyard, beach trips, nature walks and so much more. Mollie often says, "If I didn't have photos of what we did, I wouldn't remember very much at all."

It was during this time of selling memory-saving supplies, that Mollie met her future business partner, Ann Matuszak. Both Ann and Mollie, along with their other friends in the business were very disappointed when their direct sales company went into bankruptcy for the second time in 2013. It appeared to be closing their doors permanently.

Ann had an idea of starting a photo organizing business and Mollie was hooked on the idea. They both knew their customers often purchased the albums and software, but often never actually put the albums together. In fact, a photo organizing business could really give people hands on help to saving their memories. Pixologie was born three weeks later on July 25, 2013.

Mollie quit her successful healthcare career in 2014 when Pixologie opened its first location. She works with clients individually, teaches photo organization classes and has helped organize nearly one million photos since starting. She wrote "A Pixologist's Guide to Saving Family Photos," so that more people could learn how to preserve their family memories.

Lastly, Mollie has worked with the Wisconsin Senior Olympics for the past six years helping the nonprofit grow the games. Over 1200 athletes, 50 and older, compete in 20+ sporting events. It is not your grandma's senior center program! Mollie has helped the organization preserve over 3300 photos from the past two decades. Just imagine the stories and inspiration those photos will provide the athletes children and grandchildren! What is important in life? All the technological advances we've achieved that seem to keep us inside and isolated more? Or getting outside to compete, play, and enjoy life?

Mollie is married to Paul and has two children, Hannah and Alexander. She sings in her church choir and her goal is to help make the world a better place by helping people enjoy and share their memories and family histories.

www.ingramcontent.com/pod-product-compliance
Lightning Source LLC
LaVergne TN
LVHW052346100826
845147LV00012B/764

* 9 7 8 1 5 9 5 9 8 6 3 7 5 *